Whoopin' Up on Stinkin' Thinkin'

WHOOPIN' UP ON STINKIN' THINKIN'

Get Your Mind Unstuck Now!

J. MATTHEW NANCE

RESOURCE *Publications* • Eugene, Oregon

WHOOPIN' UP ON STINKIN' THINKIN'
Get Your Mind Unstuck Now!

Copyright © 2019 John Matthew Nance. All rights reserved. Except for brief quotations in critical publications or reviews, no part of this book may be reproduced in any manner without prior written permission from the publisher. Write: Permissions, Wipf and Stock Publishers, 199 W. 8th Ave., Suite 3, Eugene, OR 97401.

Resource Publications
An Imprint of Wipf and Stock Publishers
199 W. 8th Ave., Suite 3
Eugene, OR 97401

www.wipfandstock.com

PAPERBACK ISBN: 978-1-5326-8324-4
HARDCOVER ISBN: 978-1-5326-8325-1
EBOOK ISBN: 978-1-5326-8326-8

Manufactured in the U.S.A.   MAY 8, 2019

To Donnie Lanier, who at age ninety
still canoes, bird watches,
loves God, loves people,
and helps his former pastor write a better book.
Donnie, you may not know who Siri is,
but you know Christ,
and he is infinitely better!

Fit every loose thought ...
into the structure of life
shaped by Christ.

2 Corinthians 10:5 The Message

Contents

Acknowledgments / ix

1	Think About What You Are Thinking About!	/ 1
2	Tearing Down Mental Strongholds	/ 11
3	Taking Every Thought Captive	/ 25
4	Accusation Stinks!	/ 43
5	Discouragement Stinks!	/ 59
6	Stuck? Rethink for a Change!	/ 79
7	Preparing to Take Down a Stronghold	/ 91
8	Principles for Overcoming Strongholds	/ 107
9	Temptation Stinks!	/ 126
10	The Ultimate Whoopin'!	/ 143
11	Getting High on Elevated Thinking	/ 155

Bibliography / 173

Acknowledgments

ALAN DAVES, I'LL NEVER forget the day you came barreling up the driveway repeatedly honk, honk, honking your truck horn. Through the window, I saw you jumping out and running up to the door all excited about this book finding a publishing home. Thank you, Alan, for both your strong support of this book as well as your affirmation each time I diligently and passionately speak truth from God's word. You get the first copy hot off the press!

Katie Miller, thank you for your attention to the needed grammatical corrections. I have always admired your collaborative leadership style and your attention to detail.

AnnMarie Incorvaia, thank you for sharing your personal excitement over how the truths of each chapter of this book impacted your spirit, and for your suggestions on how to maximize the impact of each chapter. As your group journeys through these pages together, please let me know how God uses it to transform lives.

Donnie Lanier, you served both as a solid theological check-point and as the kind of English language master that will no longer be present without your generation among us. Sylvia would be proud of you! One day, hopefully not too soon, the Lord will say to you, "Well done . . ." In the meantime, please come see us, and let's get out in a canoe!

Justin Dennis, each week I sent you a chapter, and each week you stayed up late writing detailed, honest responses about your personal struggles in that particular area. In so doing, you helped me know how to improve each chapter to truly help people facing serious battles. As a result, the book now boldly and directly confronts deceptive mental patterns. Through straight talk and unceasing tough love, I am fighting for God to win the unseen but very real tug-of-war over your soul. My prayer is that you refuse to allow

ACKNOWLEDGMENTS

the enemy even one inch of mental ground, and that you identify and break free from all strongholds, so that you consistently enjoy the freedom and peace of mind that only Christ can give. Don't settle for any experience less than the ultimate experience; the refreshing mental clarity and awesomeness of a lavish life mysteriously empowered by Christ in you.

First Baptist Church, Dripping Springs, Texas, and Oakhill Baptist Church, Austin, Texas, you inspired me to strive for both excellence in biblical interpretation and real-life practicality while reflecting on these life-changing truths. I love the new tradition this journey started among you. Whenever you hear it being spoken, just keep putting your hand up to stop it, and keep calling it out for what it is: "Stinkin' Thinkin'!"

1

Think About What You Are Thinking About!

While living in Northwest Oklahoma City, our home was only two blocks from Lake Cobblestone. Most mornings before sunup, I would take the dogs on a one-mile walk around the lake. I would throw a tennis ball out into the lake, and the dogs enjoyed racing to fetch the ball.

The lead dog was a Labrador retriever. He was big and black, so he was named Bear. Bear Dog was always the fastest swimmer, priding himself in getting to the ball first. Though we loved Bear, he developed a disgusting habit.

Bear Dog found a place on the shore where fish would often wash up, dry out, and die. Each morning, Bear excitedly turned himself upside down, and rolled on his back on top of the dead fish. To Bear, covering his entire body with the scent of dead fish was like heaven, with the aroma lasting all day long. His very favorite part of the day was rolling around in dead, stinky fish.

You and I love stinky things as well. Some of the thoughts we allow our minds to roll around in really stink. If it were just a matter of misguided thinking, then writing a book on whoopin' up on stinkin' thinkin' would be a waste of time. The problem is our thoughts are way more than mere thoughts; they determine our personalities, behaviors, relationships, and even our entire lives.

Whoopin' Up on Stinkin' Thinkin'

For most of us, our thoughts are *reactions* to what we feel and see. However, if our thoughts are set on truth, then our thought life proactively *determines* how we see things and what we feel. Would you say your thoughts are more reactions *to* your situation or proactive creators *of* your situation?

Typically, our thoughts are merely responses to our environment and emotions. However, that is not the way the Designer intended our minds to operate. He wants our thoughts to be proactive, creative, and always set on his truth.

> *God wants our thoughts to be proactive, creative, and set on truth.*

When our thoughts are merely reactionary, our typical responses are negative things like fear, insecurity, or pride. However, when we set our minds on truth and learn to filter our surroundings through God's truth perspective, we see ourselves and our lives from a much higher perspective, which challenges and inspires us. Partner with the Thought Transformer to change your thinking, and your life *will* change!

For instance, let's say you have had a series of unfortunate events. Here's what you begin to think:

My future is going to continue just like things have been. Where is God in this? He's on vacation at the worst time in my life!

Stinkin' thinkin'!

As a result of such thinking, you mope around in self-pity, and do nothing but stare at your own lint-filled belly button. You may reach out to friends, only to seek their confirmation of how pitiful your life truly is.

The alternative: Take your situation to God, keeping your mind focused on his truth. Here's what that might look like:

Lord, You are aware that I have had some really tough-to-handle short-term setbacks. I ask you to help me realize my current condition is not permanent. I claim what you promise in Psalm 34:18, that you are close to the brokenhearted. You save those who are crushed in spirit. My heart is broken and my spirit is crushed, so draw close and save me now, Lord!

After calling the Thought Transformer into your mental process, you clean the lint out of your belly button, go out into the sunshine, and look for ways to bless and encourage the brokenhearted and the crushed in spirit. In doing so, God lifts up your spirit and begins to heal your broken heart. New

Think About What You Are Thinking About!

experiences begin entering into your life, and you realize that your future is, after all, becoming *different* from your past.

In China, where our family spent eight adventurous years, a man named Fu Yan was having terrible headaches, and nothing helped. Though going to the hospital in many places in China is not an experience anyone would want to have, he finally went to get an X-ray. The results showed a four-inch knife blade lodged in his skull! Four years prior, he had been attacked by a robber, and Fu Yan didn't even know the robber's knife blade had broken off inside his skull.

If an X-ray of your mind could somehow reveal your thoughts, what alarming things might be found there? What painful knife blades do you carry around in your head without even realizing it?

When there's pain in your brain, but you don't want to go to a mental hospital, do you tell yourself its normal? Maybe you don't even realize the thoughts you let your brain roll around in actually stink. In fact, maybe you roll your mind around in *stinkin' thinkin'* as if the thoughts were somehow helpful to you. You convince yourself that the stabbing knife pain is a strange but truly useful tool of mental torment which you need to help you rehearse your pain.

I'll never get over what happened. Stinkin' thinkin'.

My life is messed up forever because of what I did. Stinkin' thinkin'.

I failed at marriage, and now I am ashamed to see my friends. Stinkin' thinkin'.

I simply must indulge in this secret life of mine in order to feel good about myself. Stinkin' thinkin'.

I am guilty of things no one could forgive, not others, not me, and not even God. Stinkin' thinkin'.

Seems to me like I'm better than most people I know. I can't think of anyone that really has anything up on me. I've really made something of myself. Stinkin' thinkin'.

I must meet certain standards in order to feel good about myself. Stinkin' thinkin'.

I must have the approval of others to make it in life. Stinkin' thinkin'.

There aren't enough resources available to achieve this dream. There's only so much to go around. Stinkin' thinkin'.

Those who fail, including me, are unworthy. Stinkin' thinkin'.

> *Think about what you are thinking about!*

Whoopin' Up on Stinkin' Thinkin'

I cannot change. I am hopeless. I am what I am. Stinkin' thinkin'.

This is a dangerous world. Bad things might happen to me—robbery, terror, fire, or car accident. Stinkin' thinkin'.

I am finally independent of my parents and everyone else. Now I can do as I please! Stinkin' thinkin'.

Such thoughts can make it very difficult to live with the one person you must learn to live with: yourself.

You pay attention to what you eat, what you wear, how you spend money, how well you perform at work, what vehicle you drive, and how you act. However, when it comes to what you think, maybe you are not even paying attention. Your thoughts, more than anything else, determine who you are. Think about *what* you are thinking about!

The enemy makes one subtle suggestion after another, whispering thoughts into your mind that you slowly start to believe and repeat to yourself. Stinkin' thinkin' begins to trap the mind, and when something is in a trap, it cannot rest.

I feel so empty. Rejection is just so overwhelming. I've had so many clashes with just about everyone around me, and now I can't even agree with myself about anything. I am so confused. There seems to be no way out of this darkness.

Don't try changing your thoughts by self-effort or by attempting to change your behavior through sheer human willpower. Disturbing thoughts have a spiritual origin, and cannot be defeated by human means. You must cooperate with God by letting him rewire your brain. To get out of the trap, search the truth book for passages that relate to your situation, and then pray God's own word back to him. Here's what that might look like:

God, I am a mental mess. You promise in Psalm 91 that those who live within your shelter find rest. I run to you. You alone are my refuge from mental turmoil. I trust in you. I rest in you. Rescue me from every trapping thought. Cover me. Shelter me. Your truth protects my mind like armor. I will not fear or be mentally agitated. Your angels surround me wherever I go.

You feel pretty good about your struggle, until the next day when your mind falls back down into the old mental ruts laid down by the enemy. You slip back into the traps the enemy has set. Learning to have the mind of Christ within you is a process. Victory over the battle for your mind requires spending time in God's word, letting God in on your thoughts, and praying God's word back to him. When you slip back into old mental habits, it's time to do some more whoopin' up on stinkin' thinkin'.

Think About What You Are Thinking About!

Lord, it's me again. I'm being pestered by crazy thoughts once again. I choose to believe the truth of Zephaniah 3:17, that you are in the middle of my life. You are the mighty One who saves me from insanity. You quiet my mind with your larger-than-life love. Today is the continuation of me living with you constantly on my mind. The enemy is trying to bring me down, but you, Lord, according to 1 John 3:8, came to destroy the works of the devil. Destroy the strongholds in my mind God. I claim Galatians 5:1 to be true. Christ has set me free. Help me stay free. Keep me from going back into mental bondage again.

We tend to allow our brains to be left wide open, defenseless, causing our thoughts to be determined by the people and circumstances around us. It's like opening wide the top of your skull and letting any and every flying creature drop his droppings into your brain!

There is an unseen spiritual world at work around and within us. The battle for our minds is actually occurring within that invisible but very real supernatural realm. We battle against a deceptive enemy. He seeks to slip half-truths into our brain, sugar coated with seeming goodness, while the kernel within the coating is arsenic.

Though followers of Christ have God's Spirit within and cannot be demon-possessed, our thoughts can easily be demonized. Pay attention to the invisible war; look at what is happening in the spiritual, unseen realm of your mind.

The mind feasts or famines on what it focuses on. Focus your mind on a feast of truth. Whatever controls your thinking will make or break you. Be controlled by the Spirit within you. According to what you believe, so be it (Matt 9:28–29). Believe that he who began a good work in you *will* complete it. As you think in your heart, so you are (Prov 23:7). Have Christ's mind in you.

You *can* get past the thoughts that keep you in your past. Though it may seem like your life is falling apart, you *can* . . .

- choose to demolish deceptive mental strongholds and instead . . .
- hold on tight to the truths of Christ that will hold you up.

This book will show you how to replace thoughts that enslave the mind with truth-based thoughts. Time to do some whoopin' up on stinkin' thinkin'!

What do you tell yourself about yourself? It's time to consider seriously what it is you spend your

> *Whatever controls your thinking will make or break you.*

days thinking about. Examine your own self-talk for one week by keeping a journal of the things you find yourself pondering. What are you telling yourself that is not fully true?

Eugene Peterson dug into the original nuances of the New Testament language when he wrote an accurate and vivid paraphrase describing the battle for our thoughts:

> We use our powerful God-tools
> for smashing warped philosophies,
> tearing down barriers erected against the truth of God, fitting every loose thought
> and emotion
> and impulse
> into the structure of life shaped by Christ.
> (2 Cor 10:4–5 The Message Paraphrase)

Here's a key definition we will use throughout our study:

Stronghold:

An often unnoticed thought pattern based on Satan's deception, which contains truth mixed with error, finding root in your personality, determining your values and behavior, and seeking to have you act independently of God.

Without God's healing power over your mind, you may become enslaved to fear, compulsiveness, bitterness, paranoia, unforgiveness, confusion, and distrust, just to name a few stinking thoughts. The results of mental strongholds are:

... the inability to fully experience God's best
... deception accepted as truth
... a wounded spirit
... spiritual bondage

In this book, you will be guided to

- identify strongholds within your own thought life
- fight the enemy's attack supernaturally
- demolish dominating deceptions
- capture as a POW every wayward mental process
- develop the ability to think like Christ

Since the enemy's purpose of a stronghold is to have us act independently of God, tearing down a stronghold requires a declaration of dependence on God. I have written the following declaration for my own mental victory over strongholds. Living with a sense of constant dependence on God has done much to change the way I think. I share this declaration with you for your consideration. Try making a similar declaration using your own expressions.

Lord,

In a culture that lifts up high the deceptive thought of reliance on self, I choose not to be independent. Do whatever it takes in my life, my heart, my relationships, and my mind to daily reduce me down to the truth that I am utterly and completely dependent on you, even for the next breath I take. Help me not to resent but to actually embrace my dependence on you. I do hereby permanently and irreversibly before you and all humanity, make this declaration of my dependence on Christ alone.

So be it.

Whoopin' Up on Stinkin' Thinkin'

THINK ABOUT WHAT YOU ARE THINKING ABOUT!

Questions for Reflection and Discussion

1. If an X-ray could somehow reveal knife-like thoughts painfully stuck in your mind, what thoughts would it reveal?

2. In what ways do you deceive yourself?

3. Read 2 Corinthians 10:3–5 in several different translations. Write down the key principles you see in those verses:

   -
   -
   -
   -
   -

4. Of the principles you noted above, which one(s) are you . . .

Currently applying to your thought life:

In the most need of applying to your thought life:

Think About What You Are Thinking About!

5. Write your own declaration of dependence here:

6. Share with a friend what God is already beginning to do in your thought life through this study. Who will you tell?

*Thoughts like
fear, confusion, pride, distrust, anxiety,
bitterness, unforgiveness, anger,
entitlement, helplessness, and compulsiveness
eventually take root
and become stubborn strongholds.*

*Since your thoughts try to take you captive,
you must partner with God
to take your thoughts captive,
so that your mind will be captivated by Christ.*

---

*Don't be stupid
and believe all you hear;
be smart
and know
where you are headed.*

Proverbs 14:15 CEV

2

Tearing Down Mental Strongholds

OUR MINDS EASILY BECOME enslaved. Without God's healing of our minds, stinkin' thinkin' rules. Thoughts like fear, confusion, pride, distrust, anxiety, bitterness, unforgiveness, anger, entitlement, helplessness, and compulsiveness eventually take root and become stubborn strongholds.

Since your thoughts try to take *you* captive, you must partner with God to take *your thoughts* captive, so that your mind will be captivated by Christ.

> The weapons we fight with are not the weapons of the world.
> On the contrary, they have the divine power to demolish strongholds.
> (2 Cor 10:4 NIV)

The word "stronghold" describes a fortress. A stronghold is a fortified structure designed to protect what is inside and keep out all invaders. Picture the towering walls of a well-fortified castle, complete with a moat around it, well protected from external attack. Stinkin' thinkin' is just such a barricaded fort, deep within your mind.

Like a painful pimple that just won't pop, strongholds are stubborn. A mental stronghold is a thought pattern that keeps you from experiencing God's blessings. Beginning with placing distorted thoughts in your mind, Satan takes a mental foothold and quietly builds a fortress in your life. Though it is extremely difficult to conquer a stronghold, you can do all things through Christ who gives you strength.

A stronghold is like a python snake. It very quietly hums a melodic tune, hypnotizing you while it wraps itself around your mind and squeezes you into its mold. You must recognize these stinking squeezes on your mind, and call them what they are.

I'll never amount to anything! Stinkin' thinkin'!
God would never forgive me! Stinkin' thinkin'!
I'm a victim of circumstances! Stinkin' thinkin'!
Hating him is only reasonable! Stinkin' thinkin'!
I deserve my little . . . indiscretions! Stinkin' thinkin'!
I'm better than most people! Stinkin' thinkin'!
I can't change the way I think. Stinkin' thinkin'.
I am a victim. I should never trust anyone again. That way, I don't ever get hurt. Stinkin' thinkin'.
I am not wanted, not worthy, and not acceptable. Stinkin' thinkin'.

Have you ever had a barbed fishhook caught in your finger? Knowing that you have been caught by a fishhook is one thing, yet knowing how to remove the hook is quite another! Recognizing that you have a mental stronghold at work in your life is not enough. You must know how to tear it down, and then you must start the demolition. How can mental strongholds be torn down?

> *Let your mind be captivated by Christ.*

DON'T TRY TO TEAR DOWN STRONGHOLDS WITH HUMAN EFFORT

> For though we live in the world,
> we do not wage war as the world does.
> The weapons we fight with
> are not the weapons of the world.
> (2 Cor 10:4 NIV)

A stronghold is a *spiritual* force at work within your mind. It does no good to fight a spiritual problem with fleshly weapons. Within our own human flesh, we are powerless to change ourselves.

We tend to fight what we *see*. However, the battle for our minds is *unseen*. It is occurring on the *supernatural* level, as a conflict between God and Satan. Satan has set out to bring you down through his authorities in the unseen world. He has cosmic powers at work to keep you in the dark. Evil spirits in the atmosphere around you, though unseen, are very real (Eph 6:12). Though his power is not as great as God's power, it is much greater than your own power.

As a professor in Korea, I would walk up and down the aisles while teaching. While on such a walk, I noticed a female student in the very back writing the same Korean word over and over and over again, all the way down the page. The word she wrote? It was a command she was making to herself; *Pyenhwa! Pyenhwa! Change! Change!* Regardless of how many times she commanded herself to be different, she was, as we all are, powerless to change sinful nature.

There are two seemingly similar but very different sports, high jumping and pole vaulting. High jumping is fully dependent on human effort alone. Siri tells me the world high jumping record is 8.046 feet. Pole vaulting uses a force outside of human effort to catapult the same human body upward. Siri says the record for pole vaulting is twenty feet, two and a half inches! With external help, it is possible to go more than twice as high as when simply striving in our own strength!

Spiritual strongholds are built up so high in our minds that no human effort can conquer them. We *need* a force *outside* of ourselves. Bob Birdsong was a body builder in the 1970s. However, at age thirty-one he was diagnosed with testicular cancer. Facing surgery, he placed his faith in Christ. He says, "I used to boast of my own strength. Now I know God alone has power. Those who rely on human strength are gathering glory and pride for self."

> *A mental stronghold is a thought pattern that keeps us from experiencing God's blessings.*

A computer has hardware, and it has software. Your brain is your hardware. Your thoughts are the software. If you have troubling thoughts, you may think something is wrong with your brain. You may want medical help to change the hardware and solve your thought problems. What needs changed is not your hardware. Your brain is just fine. It's your software, your thoughts. However, only the Master Programmer can alter your software and change your thoughts.

When we change our thoughts, scientists tell us our brains physically change. The human brain either goes to survival mode (negative thoughts) or toward reward (positive, creative thinking). We tend to get stuck in the negative and think that's all there is. There is no hope. As we repeat hopeless thoughts, the brain creates neural pathways . . . *hopeless* . . . *hopeless* . . . *hopeless*

That thinking totally stinks!

However, when Christ comes into our lives and our thoughts are made new through the power of his Spirit within us, our brains start creating new neural pathways . . . *There is hope in Christ . . . Christ gives me hope . . . Christ himself is my hope* . . .

Some researchers assert that behavior is merely a thoughtless product of the physical brain. In reality, however, behavior is not a product of the brain but of the mind, which is *not* physical. Spiritual bondage is a thought process that results in unhealthy behavior. The bondage is not in the realm of the physical brain. Bondage cannot be broken by physical means such as surgery on the brain or the induction of chemicals into the brain. Bondage is in the mind, a nonphysical part of the human being.

Coming to a place of fully turning yourself over to the care of Christ results in an ongoing process of renewing the mind. Your mind will begin to focus on things above, not on lowly things (Rom 12:1–2; Col 3:2). The new, Spirit-empowered neural pathways will result in changed behavior.

Don't try to change your behavior with physical self-effort. Behavior that troubles you is likely a symptom of a spiritual problem; a mental stronghold may be at work within you. Partner with God. Get his reprogramming power at work changing your thoughts so that you begin developing the mind of Christ. Your behavior will then follow your newly created mind, instead of following the old ways of your human flesh.

As a man thinks, so he is (Prov 23:7 KJV). There is a war going on for your attention. The focus of the war is the flesh versus the spirit. We walk around in a physical world, yet we can have victory only if we become spiritual. Let's get spiritual! Learn to see life from the spiritual point of view, and live for the unseen yet ultimate reality of God himself, who is Spirit.

Practically, how do we focus on the spiritual more than the physical? What spiritual weapons do we use to conquer the flesh?

USE SUPERNATURAL WEAPONS TO CONQUER STRONGHOLDS

> The weapons we fight with . . .
> have the divine power
> to demolish strongholds.
> (2 Cor 10:4 NIV)

The word "power" in this verse is the word *dunamis*, from which we get our word "dynamite." Picture the explosive power of God Almighty at work in your thought life! Now imagine that the One who has the power to raise the dead has been invited by you to change your thoughts. Right now experience the re-creative power of God Almighty flooding into your mind and blasting away those strongholds that were previously ruining your life.

God's great gushes of living water are washing away all your stinkin' thinkin' and replacing it with his truth and light. From your inner thoughts outward, you are becoming new in Christ.

The fight is not only God's work. It is ours. He has placed *his* weapons of divine power in *our* hands for us to demolish the strongholds in our lives. What are some of these weapons?

Prayer

If God answered all the prayers you pray, what difference would it make? Are you praying? Are there specific areas of your life in which you are experiencing a mental tug of war? Prayerless living leads to a defeated mind-set. God's word says you have not because you ask not. Pray and ask God for help! If your prayers go unanswered, search your motives for asking God. Do you pray sincerely asking God to change your heart and mind?

Fasting

Like nothing else, fasting puts the spirit above the flesh. A stronghold is a dependency on something that is taking the place of dependence on God. Fasting creates total dependency on God, exposing the God-substitutes of your life.

Have you allowed something to be elevated to the point of putting your dependence on it rather than on God? It could be a person, a place, a position, a pleasure, power, or even a plaything. If it takes more of your focus than you give to God, it is a stronghold, a God-substitute. Fasting, when done from a contrite heart, will get you back to total dependence on God.

Dependence on the Holy Spirit

Do you grieve the Spirit by not listening to him? Does your daily decision-making process allow time and space for seeking the input of the Holy Spirit, even in the seemingly "little" decisions? When the Spirit speaks to you, do you quench the Spirit by refusing to obey? Are you fully dead to self and fully alive to the Spirit?

> *He has placed his weapons of divine power in our hands for us to demolish strongholds.*

God's Word

It is not possible to have thoughts steadily fixed on God and at the same time have a mind that is not at rest. "You will keep in perfect peace all who trust in you, all whose thoughts are fixed on you" (Isa 26:3 NLT). Saturate your mind with God's word and you will be protected from stinkin' thinkin'. God's word will reprogram your mind, filling you with life and joy.

Spiritual Songs

Music is much more powerful than we realize. It can determine your mood, your thoughts, your beliefs and actions, yet most of us listen undiscerningly. We turn on the radio and sing right along with that old country song, "O Lord, it's hard to be humble, when you're perfect in every way." Is the music you listen to bringing you closer to God? Is it breaking down or building up strongholds in your mind? Does the music you listen to focus on the spirit or on the flesh? Find a positive, encouraging Christian station and put it on your preset. Keep worship music loaded on your playlist.

Godly Mentors

During our twenty years serving as missionaries in East Asia, Bill Fudge was my mentor. When we were sensing God doing something new in our lives, I talked with Bill, and God would use him to open the way into life's next chapter.

That proved to be true even after returning to the United States. Despite the gnats, we had enjoyed five challenging years pastoring in Southern Georgia. When Bill came from Oklahoma to be our guest speaker one weekend, I confided in Bill that I had a constant desire to serve God in a more multicultural context. I asked him to pray that God would take that desire away from me.

To my surprise, Bill said, "Matthew, are you walking with God?"

"Yes," I replied.

"Then I will *not* pray for God to take that desire away from you. You are delighting yourself in God. I will pray that he gives you the desires of your heart." And with that, he fell quiet. End of subject. Almost. Within six months, we found ourselves living in Oklahoma City, pastoring an inner city church in a multicultural context, including a network of five ethnic congregations!

> *Do you have someone who challenges your stinkin' thinkin'?*

My way of thinking was actually prohibiting what God wanted for our lives. Bill called out my *stinkin' thinkin'*.

Having a godly mentor makes all the difference between stinkin' thinkin' and a life of adventure with God. Do you have someone who challenges your *stinkin' thinkin'*? Are there a few people who need you to be their mentor, to help them do some *whoopin' up on stinkin' thinkin'*?

The Armor of God

Ephesians 6 tells us that if we are to stand firm against the strategies of the devil, God's truth must become like a belt to us, holding us together. God's righteousness must become like body armor to us. The goods news must become like shoes carrying us through life with God's peace. Faith must become like a shield stopping the enemy's arrows. Salvation must become like a helmet, protecting our thoughts. The sword of the word of God must become our weapon of offense against deception (Eph 6:10–17).

Prayer, fasting, God's word, dependence on God's Spirit within you, scriptural songs, godly mentors, and God's armor: these are some of the weapons with which we fight. It *is* a *fight*; an ongoing struggle, one in which you can never let up. Are you serious about launching an ongoing campaign to take every thought captive and make it obey Christ?

How can mental strongholds be brought down? Don't try tearing down strongholds with human effort. Use supernatural weapons to conquer strongholds. There is another consideration.

TARGET SPECIFIC STRONGHOLDS IN YOUR LIFE

> We fight . . . to demolish strongholds.
> (2 Cor 10:4 NIV)

The word for "demolish" in the original language of the New Testament is *kathairountes*, from which we get our word "catharsis," or cleansing. The human mind needs cleansing! The New Testament word is kin to an Old Testament word used to describe the tearing down of idols.

Strongholds are idols of the mind. They are rooms within you locked away from God's presence. Strongholds do not need to be remodeled. They do not need to have the locks on their doors changed. They must be torn down, one at a time. Take God's wrecking ball and demolish all thought patterns that are not from him!

> *The human mind needs cleansing!*

Laura Klock's life was like a ticking time bomb ready to explode. She knew that her birth was not planned. She said, "I am a mistake." (*Stinkin' thinkin'!*) She discovered that if she drank, she could be this other person. (*Stinkin' thinkin'!*)

By age sixteen, she was pregnant and had a secret abortion. She saw her dead child and began weeping. Guilt, shame, and low self-worth filled her thoughts. She would zoom away from it all on a fast motorcycle, even setting the land speed record.

During college, she went from one drug to the next, one relationship to the next. Then she met Brian, who invited her to church and to faith in Christ. Finally, she accepted God's love and truth. Now she says, "I am not a mistake. I am part of God's plan!" Her mental strongholds were torn down by the power of Christ!

Tearing Down Mental Strongholds

A stronghold stands at a specific spot in your mind, and is not easily penetrated by outside influence, partly because it is camouflaged from human vision. You and I will rationalize, trying to convince ourselves that the stronghold is acceptable. It takes spiritual vision to recognize a specific stronghold for what it actually is.

A stronghold, though often unseen, actually occupies a particular place in your life. For example, you may be living in self-pity and envy, thinking, "Everybody else in this world has more than I have." *Stinkin' thinkin'!* Such a dominant thought in your life becomes deeply rooted as your life's theme.

Such a "theme-of-life" thought is a stronghold. It leads to behavior which does not honor God, does not build up others, and does not bring blessings your way. With the strongholds of self-pity and envy (not to mention pride), you end up acting on this premise: "Even if I have to beg, borrow, or steal, I'll do whatever it takes to get what I deserve."

We typically have more than one stronghold in our lives, and dealing with them shotgun style does not work well. We end up splattering the walls of many strongholds, just stirring up the fort guards a bit, while not digging out by the roots any of the strongholds. Strongholds must be identified, uprooted, and demolished one by one.

In a time of prayer, ask God to reveal to you any and all strongholds in your life. Some areas mentioned below describe behaviors. Strongholds are thoughts not behaviors. However, the behavior shows evidence that there is some kind of stronghold supporting it. If you exhibit the behavior, ask God why you are acting that particular way. *God, come show me what's going on in my mind!* He will show up on site with insight.

In some cases, a circumstance that is no fault of your own creates twisted thinking in your mind. You may not be able to rewind and erase the circumstance, but you can determine your reaction to it.

If you have trouble identifying your own strongholds, write down what you tell yourself about yourself, about others, about this world, and about God. Dialogue with your spiritual mentor or pastor will also help you identify strongholds.

You may fear that if you take this inventory, you will find so many strongholds that you don't know where to begin. Take the inventory once without overthinking it. Deal first with only the issues that readily surface. Take the inventory again later, and perhaps other areas will be revealed to you.

Whoopin' Up on Stinkin' Thinkin'

CHECKLIST FOR STRONGHOLDS, STRONGHOLD-RELATED BEHAVIORS, AND STRONGHOLD-PRODUCING INCIDENTS

Emotional

___ anger
___ worry
___ fear
___ depression
___ negativity
___ loneliness
___ bitterness
___ insecurity
___ unforgiveness
___ despair
___ suspicion
___ rejection (of self or others)
___ excess introversion
___ excess extroversion
___ self-deprecation
_____

Spiritual

___ guilt
___ judgmental spirit
___ prejudice
___ pride
___ resenting God
___ resenting others
___ doubts
___ hypocrisy
___ depend on "luck"
___ participating in cults
___ palm reading
___ visit a spiritist
_____

Physical

___ suicidal
___ cutting
___ addiction
___ eating disorder
___ psychologically-based ailment
_____

Relational

___ serial divorce
___ meanness
___ envy
___ self-reliance
___ hatred
___ selfishness
___ irritability
___ fear of commitment
___defensiveness
___ People pleasing
_____

unable to get along with . . .
___ same sex
___ opposite sex

Sexual

___ sex outside marriage
___ sex before marriage
___ enjoy pain infliction
___ homosexuality
___ lesbianism
___ abortion
___ frigidity
_____

Whoopin' Up on Stinkin' Thinkin'

sex abuse . . .
___ victim
___ perpetrator
rape . . .
___ victim
___ perpetrator

Financial

___ workplace theft
___ gambling
___ stealing
___ greed
___ shopaholic
___ self-induced poverty
___ excess debt
___ lack of giving
___ hoarding
_____

Mental

___ tormented
___ no will to live
___ inner unrest
___ low coping ability
___ indecisiveness
___ stuck in life
___ distracted
___ easily confused
_____

TEARING DOWN MENTAL STRONGHOLDS

Questions for Reflection and Discussion

1. What is your frequency of evaluating the worth of the things you most often think about?

   ___ often

   ___ seldom

   ___ never

2. Read 2 Corinthians 10:3–5. After taking the inventory, what have you identified as strongholds in your life?

3. Of the spiritual weapons mentioned in the chapter, what weapons work best for you?

4. Memorize God's word. Let your mind dwell on God's truth. In the space provided, write out each of the verses below. Share with a friend what God is doing in your thought life through these verses:

   2 Corinthians 10:4

   Romans 12:1–2

   Colossians 3:2

   Isaiah 26:3

> *Guard your heart
> above everything else,
> for it determines
> the course of your life.*
>
> *Proverbs 4:23 NLT*

3

Taking Every Thought Captive

We lived in Georgia for five years, below the gnat line. Those of you from Georgia know exactly what I'm talking about. There is an invisible line running east and west at Macon, Georgia. Above the line, gnats don't care to live. Below the line, they thrive. And in the south part of that hot, humid state, they thrive on human sweat!

While I mowed our one-acre lawn with a push mower, the gnats had plenty of time to enjoy my ears, nose, and eyelids. At first I tried to keep them away. Over time, I noticed that the local men had learned to negotiate with the gnats, allowing them to land, but not go too far. So I also began taking that more reasonable approach.

I told the gnats, "You can have the outer and most of the inside parts of my ears, but if you go toward the ear canal, I'm coming after you! And those of you on my eyelids, you have to stay on the outer part of my eyelids where I will allow you to rest and drink my sweat, but if you crawl toward the pink inner part, you are in trouble. Those of you on my nose hairs, you are acceptable where you are, but if you go up either nostril, I will blow you out so fast you won't know what hit you!"

> *Oh, the mental pests we tolerate!*

Nasty gnats are a lot like pesky thoughts we try to swat away, only for them to come right back again. Oh the mental pests we tolerate! We put up with things much worse than gnats. Pestering thoughts crawl around in our minds irritating us to no end—anger, fear, self-deprecation, pride, guilt, defensiveness, lust, shame, hopelessness, greed, and worthlessness. Why do we put up with such harmful creatures torturing us to insanity?

As we negotiate territory with them, they begin to set up camp in our minds. When we *accommodate their intrusion*, we are actually *approving their inclusion* as a part of who we are, even if we attempt to enforce supposed limits on them. And before you know it, the thoughts we tolerate begin to dominate.

Since your thoughts try to take you captive, you must partner with God for mental victory, so that you take captive every mental stronghold, resulting in your mind becoming captivated by Christ alone.

By whoopin' up on stinkin' thinkin', you will acquire the tools to help you develop the mind of Christ, resulting in his great joy and your peace of mind. You *can* train yourself to recognize and take captive your own stinkin' thinkin'.

> *The thoughts we tolerate begin to dominate.*

"This is just who I am. I can't change!" *Stinkin' thinkin'!*

"I brought my life to the point where I am today. I am a self-made man!" *Stinkin' thinkin'!*

"She's hot! I don't care if we both have someone else. I have to have her!" *Stinkin' thinkin'!*

"Most people out there are ashamed of me. Better just stay home." *Stinkin' thinkin'!*

"In my humble opinion, I am always right." *Stinkin' thinkin'!*

"This gossip gig is really fun! Let's see what else I can say about her!" *Stinkin' thinkin'!*

"I have too many limitations to amount to much of anything!" *Stinkin' thinkin'!*

Do you find your mind dwelling on a particular mental message? Are you stuck on that specific thought, like a song playing repeatedly all day long, a song that no one else is hearing but you? Is it like you have earbuds in your ears, and someone other than you has programmed the message that is repeated constantly in your mind? A mental stronghold may have taken you captive.

> We use our powerful God-tools
> for smashing warped philosophies,
> tearing down barriers erected against the truth of God,

> fitting every loose thought and emotion and impulse
> into the structure of life shaped by Christ.
> (2 Cor 10:4–5 The Message Paraphrase)

Read that again, slowly thinking about each phrase.

Imagine a houseguest you invite in to your home. At first, the relationship seems needed. You've wanted something new in your life. Having the guest feels nice and cozy. However, he slowly starts taking over your family's life. Your guest tells you he is taking the family car and will be back sometime later.

That night, when you are watching a program, he changes the TV to a different program and says, "I'm turning it up to maximum volume because I'm almost deaf." As you start to talk over the program, he says, "Shh! Be quiet!" This person you have invited in as a guest has become your master, making you his servant. Strongholds of the mind are a lot like unwanted guests who hold their host captive with their unreasonable and unwanted demands.

A stronghold is a recurring thought that is often partially true yet partially false, and is designed by the enemy to put your mind in bondage and destroy your potential to live the life God has for you.

Run to Christ, the bondage breaker! Let him whoop up on your stinkin' thinkin'! Over time, the mind of Christ can be developed within you, resulting in sanity, serenity, and sound thinking. Sow a thought, and you reap an action. Sow an action, and you reap a habit. Sow a habit, and you reap a character. Sow a character, and you reap a destiny.

> *A stronghold is designed by the enemy to put your mind in bondage and destroy the life God has for you.*

How can we take every thought captive? What are some common ideologies of our day that are mixed with both truth and lies, leading to mental captivity? What voices of reason speak to us today making human logic seem like the proper basis for a sound mind? What can be done to think as Christ would think?

Christ's teachings were not the cultural norms of his day. The majority of the world in Christ's day did not accept his teachings. The same is true today. Following Christ often means choosing Christ over culture. How can we learn to swim upstream in a world pulling us downstream?

Here are four essentials for taking every thought captive.

CLEANSE THE MIND OF HUMAN IDEOLOGIES

> We use God's mighty weapons,
> not worldly weapons,
> to knock down the strongholds of human reasoning
> and to destroy false arguments.
> We destroy every proud obstacle
> that keeps people from knowing God.
> (2 Cor 10:4–5a NLT)

The words "human reasoning" come from the New Testament Greek word *logismous*, from which we get our word "logic." Logic-based arguments can come across as irrefutable. One concept is accepted as true, then another concept is placed on top of that one, in what appears to be a solid argument. In reality, the entire line of reasoning may be nothing more than a house built with a deck of cards. Human reasoning often does not stand up to the ultimate truth found in God's revelation of himself.

> *Human reasoning lifts itself up as the ultimate authority.*

God's thoughts are nothing like man's reasoning. His ways are far beyond anything humans can imagine. As the Supreme Intelligent One residing above all galaxies, his thoughts are way higher than puny mortal "reason" (Isa 55:8–9).

When something seems reasonable, it often becomes an "ism" or an "ology." For more on this phenomenon, just read the book *Isms and Ologies: All the Movements, Ideologies, and Doctrines That Have Shaped Our World*. If you have trouble with insomnia, you will find the book helpful.

Placing our trust in human ideologies prevents us from fully experiencing who God is. Human reasoning lifts itself up as the ultimate authority, yet there is so much we don't know and understand. Human ideologies take pride in mankind's intelligence, yet God opposes the proud. Here are some common ideologies widely accepted today. None of them have a valid place for the One true God within their ideology.

Humanism

Humanism is the idea that we should respect the goodness of human nature. Mankind is thought to be making himself better and better. The humanistic worldview says mankind has the capability of making this world a better place, and Humanism says that we are actually doing so.

There is a fatal flaw in such thinking. History proves clearly that "all have sinned and fallen short of the glory of God" (Rom 3:23 NLT). While it is true that God created man as good, and man does indeed have the potential for good, sin has messed up everything. Once sin entered the world, every human being is born with a nature depraved by sin (Rom 3:9–12; 1 John 1:8–10).

> *We use our God-tools for smashing warped philosophies.*

Humankind may be advancing in technology, but are our relationships with each other improving? Does history point to man as primarily good? Are divorces, physical abuse, rape, murder, theft, and war all decreasing over time?

The good possibility within humanity has been tainted by a self-centered bent inherited from the first humans. Many "beneficial" technological advances created by man have often been used for the detriment of individuals, the destruction of ethnic groups, and the abuse of the earth.

Is your view of mankind based on humanism? What do you believe is the basic nature of mankind; good or bad? Do you have to teach a baby to be selfish, or is he just innately selfish? Can we become good on our own? Do we have the capacity to make this world a utopia? How is that working out now?

"Isn't life all about us anyway?" *Stinkin' thinkin'!*

Darwinism

Darwinism says that random events set off a chain of life, which has slowly morphed into different forms. Each form has become more intricate. Humans are seen as a step in evolution, having originated without intelligent design.

It takes an incredible amount of faith to believe that the complex world in which we live was created by chance and is being held together by highly advanced principles which had no origin or intelligent design behind them. It's like believing that a wind could blow through a junk yard and create a 747 jet!

For those of us who live with eyes open, there is obviously intelligent design all around. "In the beginning, God created the heavens and the earth" (Gen 1:1).

To what degree have you bought in to the idea that this world has come about by a random sequence of events, which set in motion a progression of life forms, each becoming more complex?

"Well, maybe our existence has more to do with the biological evolving of life forms over time than with anything else. Who's to say?" *Stinkin' thinkin'!*

Materialism

Materialism says that ultimate reality is what you see and touch here and now. If there is any other reality, such as a spiritual realm, materialism says it subjugates itself to the physical realm of life. Scientific research and its conclusions, according to materialism, define the ultimate realities of this world.

However, the Bible says, "God is Spirit, and those who worship him must worship in spirit and in truth" (John 4:24 NLT). God is ultimate reality and he is spiritual in nature. We come to know ultimate reality when our spirits, our soulful true selves, become connected with God, accepting as truth what he says to be true.

> *We were made for another world.*

This world is not all there is! Deep down, we know there is something more to life than mere biological existence. We long to discover what on earth we are here for. There is a yearning for eternity in our hearts. C. S. Lewis said, "If we find ourselves with a desire that nothing in this world can satisfy, the most probable explanation is that we were made for another world."[1]

Do you tend to live for this world, or do you live with eternity in view? Would an observer of your life conclude that you believe more in material reality than you do in the spiritual dimension of life? Do you spend more time and energy on things that will be gone when your life is over, or on

---

1. www.goodreads.com/quotes

things that make a difference in eternity? Do material things have a stronghold on your life?

"This world is all there is." *Stinkin' thinkin'!*

Universalism

Universalism says that god is whatever you perceive him, her, or it to be. All spiritual roads, according to universalism, lead up the same mountain. What matters is your sincerity. Universalists say everyone putting their faith in something is going to heaven.

"Jesus said, 'I am the way, the truth, and the life. No one can come to the Father except through me" (John 14:6 NLT). Universalism is a beautiful thought, one which we want to be true. Even God does not want anyone to perish and be eternally separated from himself. He wants all to be saved. God provided the way for all people to know him and be with him. That way is Jesus, and he is the only way to heaven. *Whosoever will* may come to him.

When you are asked for the password before entry into a bank safety deposit box, can you put in any password you like? No. There is only one password that will get you in, and that password is predetermined by the owner of the deposit box. Try this: stand there and have a hissy fit, saying, "Any password ought to get me in!" Of course, that would be ridiculous.

You have an account with God, which is in the red. Because of your sin, you owe a huge debt to God so big that you cannot pay it. However, Jesus paid the debt you owe God, and if you ask him to do so, he will forgive your debt and give you himself as the password access into life with the Father God now and forever. There is no other access to heaven except Jesus.

The last time someone told you of the death of someone you did not know, did you instantly say, "Well, they are in a better place now"? Such a belief is universalism. Do you believe that everyone, regardless of whether or not they trusted Christ for salvation, is going to heaven? *Stinkin' thinkin'!*

Hedonism

Hedonism builds on materialism, by saying that since this world is all there is, if it feels good, do it. It can't be wrong, when it feels so right. Eat, drink, and be merry, for tomorrow you die.

On some tomorrow we will stand before our Creator Judge. On one of these tomorrows coming very soon, each of us will give an account before the Lord concerning how we lived our lives. Did we live for him or for ourselves? "Each of us will give a personal account to God" (Rom 14:12 NLT). "There is a path before each person that seems right, but it ends in death" (Prov 14:12 NLT).

> *If it involves pain and suffering, do you ignore God's will?*

Does physical pleasure govern your life? Do you live according to what makes you happy, ignoring God's will if it involves pain and suffering? Do you follow your mind's impulses instead of God's principles? *Stinkin' thinkin'!*

Relativism

Relativism is the cousin of universalism, saying that there are no moral absolutes. Each man should do whatever is right in his own mind. Live and let live. What's true for you may not be true for me.

Can you imagine what would become of law and order if relativism was actually carried out by our police and courts of law? Someone found guilty of murder could simply say, "Murder may be wrong for you, but it's not wrong for me. Therefore, I hereby declare that I am not guilty of any wrong."

During Noah's day, every man did what was right in his own eyes. People became so wicked that God restarted civilization with Noah and his family.

"What sorrow for those who say that evil is good and good is evil, that dark is light and light is dark, that bitter is sweet and sweet is bitter" (Isa 5:21 NLT). God is righteous and holy, and he has declared moral absolutes in his word.

Do you live by your own rules? Though other people play with fire and get burned, do you think you can play with it and not get burned? *Stinkin' thinkin'!*

Self-Reliance

Self-reliance says, "If it's going to be, it's up to me. The greatest love of all is learning to love myself. Life is all about my own happiness. God may be somewhere out there, but I am the captain of my ship. He can be my part-time copilot if he wants."

Not only does self-reliance alienate a person from God, it also isolates people from each other. The nation of North Korea has as its national motto self-reliance, and as a result, North Koreans are perhaps the most isolated, miserable people on the planet.

Americans pride ourselves in lone individualism, singing, "I did it my way," and getting the applause of others as we live in a self-reliant way.

The truth is we need God. We need each other as well. God has created us to be dependent on him and codependent on each other.

"Trust in the Lord with all your heart; do not depend on your own understanding. Seek his will in all you do, and he will show you which path to take" (Prov 3:5 NLT).

When you are making a decision, what is the first thing you do? Do you simply ask yourself what you should do? Does your own common sense guide you? Do you feel you have the best understanding of anyone as to how your life should be carried out? *Stinkin' thinkin'!*

Religion

This one may surprise you. How can religion be a negative thing? By definition, religion is man's attempt to reach God. Jesus was sick and tired of dead religion. He condemned those who were religious, because in their pride, they thought that they had arrived at a place of God's acceptance by their own good works or inherit merit.

> *What the Father God longs for you is not religion. It's relationship with him.*

What the Father God longs for you is not religion. It is relationship with him. There is a world of difference between the two.

Religion says that man's efforts can bring about spiritual healing and wholeness. Thousands of years of history have shown the utter futility of religion. Only those without sin can come to him. Are you without sin? We simply cannot make ourselves presentable to God because he is completely holy, without sin.

Religion comes up with strict rules in an effort to keep man from sinning, while ignoring the true condition of man's heart. "Regulations—'Do not handle, Do not taste, Do not touch'... human precepts and teachings—these have indeed an appearance of wisdom in promoting self-made religion and asceticism and severity to the body, but they are of no value in stopping the indulgence of the flesh" (Col 2:21–23 ESV).

Do you live a religious life so that others will consider you to be a moral person? Do you think that following a legalistic list will somehow make your heart pure before God? Do you inflict a self-made code of conduct on others as a test of their heart's connection with God? *Stinkin' thinkin'!*

The first step in taking every thought captive for Christ is cleansing the mind of human ideologies which set themselves up as the ultimate authority in your life. None of these ideologies we have examined place the Lord on the throne of your life. Only with him on the throne will you be free of stinkin' thinkin'. Here's the second step toward taking every thought captive for Christ.

STOP DEPENDING ON REASON

> We use God's mighty weapons, not worldly weapons,
> to knock down the strongholds of human reasoning
> and to destroy false arguments.
> We destroy every proud obstacle
> that keeps people from knowing God.
> (2 Cor 10:4–5a NLT)

A reader of these verses in the original Greek language would catch the nuance of the language and envision human reason having lifted itself up as the highest authority, and then the reader would watch as God's dynamite blows human reason to smithereens, reducing it to rubble on the ground.

Why do we depend so much on human reason? Why is every decision made by using good ol' common sense? Is common sense what caused Noah to build an ark? Is reason what caused Daniel to refuse to worship the king, even though his refusal sent him to the lion's den? Is common sense what caused Jesus to be quiet when falsely accused and illegally killed?

> *The will of God is often not at all reasonable.*

It is time to tear down the idea that Christ followers should be reasonable and live by their own common sense. The will of God is often *not at all* reasonable. Why in the world would a young couple take their two kids to the other side of the world and live among those in poverty and oppression, just for the sake of sharing the gospel? That's not reasonable. Why would an executive quit a six-figure job and start giving his millions away for the sake of an unseen future kingdom of some sort? No common sense in that at all!

Sometimes, in fact all of the time, we must disregard human logic and simply go with God. Reason can be used as a means of rebellion from God's will for you. We must quit singing along with Fleetwood Mac, "You can go your own way," and start singing the old gospel song "Wherever He Leads, I'll Go." Stop trying to figure everything out! Reason can deceive you into following some voice other than God's voice.

The voice of *self* says, "What really matters is my own happiness." *Stinkin' thinkin'!* Watch out! It's easy to listen to your own voice and deceive yourself into thinking you are hearing God's voice. When you come to Christ, your self-centered bent is not instantly erased. You must train your mind to listen to Christ's voice, letting it come through loud and clear over the voice of reasonable self.

> *Satan points out your faults to bring you down. Run to God's grace!*

The voice of *society* says, "Let this world around you mold you into a more acceptable and reasonable way of thinking. Listen to the ads, to peer pressure, and to the lifestyles of the rich and famous on TV. We will tell you the natural and reasonable way to live it up!" *Stinkin' thinkin'!*

The voice of *Satan* says, "You don't really believe that archaic idea that the devil is real, do you? I mean, get real! Even if he were for real, it's the twenty-first century! What influence could the devil possibly have on you anyway? Do you think he would even notice your existence?" *Stinkin' thinkin'!*

The voice of *sexuality* says, "Let your imagination run wild. Enter into whatever mental fantasies you can create. You are a sexual human. It's only reasonable that you use whatever it takes to get you where you know you can go. You don't even need a real physical companion. Just use your imagination!" *Stinkin' thinkin'!*

We have been duped by the devil into thinking that meaningful sexuality can be found through a mere recreational sexual encounter, or in the virtual world, without the work involved in a lifetime spousal commitment. Whoopin' up on such stinkin' thinkin' involves "casting down imaginations" (2 Cor 10:5 KJV).

Peter said to Jesus, in essence, "Let's be reasonable, Lord. You don't really have to go to the cross." Jesus said to Peter, "Get thee behind me Satan!" Be like Jesus and refuse to live by human reason. Recognize, as Jesus did, that attempts to pressure you into reasonable living are satanic in origin.

Human pride raises the banner of reason and builds strongholds of thoughts from it. Even now as I proofread this, a voice is telling me, "Matthew, what you have written here is not balanced. You must be more reasonable!"

Can reason and faith coexist as coequals in a person's inner guidance system? Common sense says, yes, they can. However, let's pose the question another way. Can self-reliance and God-reliance coexist as equals? Deep down we know clearly that we must choose one or the other.

Self-reliance depends on human reason; The God-reliant person moves forward though life solely by believing that God knows what he is doing, while not trusting in self's understanding. True knowledge of God humbles man to live by faith, not by reason. One or the other must be chosen as your source of guidance. Which do you choose?

How can you take captive every thought? First, cleanse the mind of human ideologies. Second, stop depending on human reason. Here is the third step.

CAPTURE EVERY UNTRUE THOUGHT AS A P.O.W.

> We take captive every thought
> to make it obedient to Christ.
> (2 Cor 10:5 NIV)

Taking POWs captive is a team activity. These verses in 2 Corinthians focusing on whoopin' up on stinkin' thinkin' are written with the plural "we." Paul, the coach, has rounded up the team and now he is giving the team strategy.

"Alright everybody. Listen up! Here's what we do to win. We work together! When you approach the enemy, team up with each other and take the enemy together as our captive. Don't try to defeat the enemy as if you are a team of one. It's 'we' not 'me.'"

Who has your back when it comes to spiritual warfare? Who is partnering with you toward victory as you honestly share your points of vulnerability and ask for help? Who is holding you accountable for taking every thought captive?

How serious are you about a catharsis of your thought life? How tolerant are you of stinkin' thinkin'?

Would you be willing to let rats live in your house? Of course not! What would you do? You would set traps, put out poison, even shoot them dead if necessary!

Some of your thoughts stink. They are rats. They don't need to be urged to leave with a soft broom. They need to be tortured and put to death.

Some of your thoughts are traitors, pretending to be on your side of life. Traitors should not be tolerated. Some of your thoughts deceive you, like the thought you may have right now that you have no need for catharsis of your thought life!

Mike Singletary was a player on the Chicago Bears in the 1980s and '90s and later coached the 49ers. He said,

> I had everything. Everybody told me I had everything, and I said, "Yeah, I do." Yet football glory left me really empty . . . the loneliest I've ever been.
>
> I even prayed, "God, why don't you use me anymore?" God said, "Mike, how can I use you when you take all the glory? How can I use you when you won't live for me or forgive your own father?" Then God began to take away things I was looking at and things I was thinking about. I finally humbled myself before God. Now Christ means everything to me.[2]

To capture every untrue thought, start an honest conversation with God about the things you think about most. Ask him to help you think about what you are thinking about. Revisit the stronghold inventory from the previous chapter.

> *Start an honest conversation with God about the things you think about most.*

Keep a daily journal tracking your actual thoughts through the day. Do so for a long enough period of time to get

---

2. Youtube Mike Singletary: Christ Means Everything

Whoopin' Up on Stinkin' Thinkin'

an accurate read on your thought life. Get with a few people who are also serious about developing the mind of Christ, and team together to take captive some really stinkin' thinkin'!

There is a final step in taking every thought captive.

PUT EVERY THOUGHT UNDER OBEDIENCE TO CHRIST

> We take every thought captive
> to make it obedient to Christ.
> (2 Cor 10:5 NIV)

Once a wayward thought is taken captive, that thought must be replaced, or else a vacuum is created in your brain. What happens if you take away all untrue, impure, negative thoughts, and leave nothing to fill the vacuum? You are asking for trouble!

> *Read the red letters of Christ's words. Circle his commands, and fill your mind and life with obeying him.*

Jesus told a story about one demon that was cast out. Seven demons returned, found the house empty, and infested it! Don't let your brain be found empty. Fill it with obedience to Christ.

Get a red-letter edition of the Bible. The red letters are the words of Christ. Read the Bible through, following the red letters. Circle or highlight the commands of Christ. Focus your life, out of love for him and others, on following the commands of Christ.

When he says, "Go," you go! When he says, "Give," you give. When he says, "Speak a blessing," you speak a blessing. When he says, "Put on the whole armor," you start suiting up. When he says, "Fight for your family," fight! When he says, "Be holy," be holy. When he says, "Serve," you serve. Saturate your mind with a consuming desire to know and *do* the will of Christ.

While pastoring in Georgia, I spent a year studying the red letters spoken by Christ. I divided his words into five main categories, and began preaching through each category. I noticed, however, that I kept pushing the most voluminous category to last, and I even began thinking that category did not need to be preached.

The category? Jesus' clash with the Pharisees. My reasoning for ignoring that part of what Jesus said? It presented a version of Jesus different than the one I imagined as a boy in Sunday School. Jesus was supposed to be this really meek and mild person. As an adult and a pastor, a fresh read of the teachings of Christ revealed a side of Jesus new to me.

Jesus got *mad* at the Pharisees, consistently. Everyone saw the Pharisees as the best religious leaders, as great examples to follow. Jesus told them and everyone in earshot that the Pharisees were prideful phonies, venomous vipers even. Yikes!

To discover this new side of Jesus was one thing, but if I were to continue preaching through the red letters, religious phonies in the church might get mad at me! (That thought shows there is within me a fear of what people think. Alright, all of you reading this may now say to me out loud together, *Stinkin' thinkin', Matthew!*)

No, I did not ignore the largest portion of Jesus' words. Yes, I did preach about Jesus' clash with the Pharisees, and it was one of the most powerful seasons of preaching ever. Yes, it did get some people mad, but hearts started changing, and so did the church culture. I even wrote a book about Jesus' encounters with the Pharisees, called *Are You for Real?*

A story is told of a football game tied at twenty-one to twenty-one. The fans on both sides were going wild, each side cheering for their team. Right then a little dog ran out on to the field, and stopped the play. The players tried to catch the critter, but he was too fast. The fans all tried calling the dog off the field, but the poor little pup heard so many voices, he ran here and there, not knowing which way to go.

Finally, the announcer got on the mic and said, "Would everyone please sit down. Would you please be completely quiet? Thank you. Now would the owner, and only the owner, please call your dog off the field." A little ol' grandmother's voice was heard. "Sweetie! Sweetie!" Instantly, the dog singled out the voice of his master, and knew exactly where to go!

There are so many voices calling out to you today. Trying to follow multiple voices leads to nothing but confusion. Single out the voice of the Master! Your mind will become clear, and you will know exactly what he wants you to think, and where he wants you to go. No more crazy running here and there! Your mind will have the peace of Christ.

Whoopin' Up on Stinkin' Thinkin'

TAKING EVERY THOUGHT CAPTIVE

Questions for Reflection and Discussion

Ever had a house guest that just would not leave? Ever had a recurring thought that just continued to pester you?

The chapter you just read reveals eight common current ideologies. Were you surprised to find yourself agreeing with some of these ideologies? Which ones? What changes are you considering in your own ideologies?

Read 2 Corinthians 10:4–5 NLT. Paraphrase the two verses using your own words:

Each ideology is a particular lens through which the world is seen; a worldview. How would you define a biblical worldview for a follower of Christ?

Review the four voices of reason covered in the middle of the chapter. How have any or all of these voices of reason affected your thinking?

1. Self

2. Society

3. Satan

4. Sexuality

Has God ever asked you to do something that wasn't reasonable? What would your response be if he were to do so now?

Reflect on the following verses. Memorize them. Share with a friend what God is doing in your thought life through these verses:

Proverbs 3:5

John 4:24

Romans 8:31

John 14:6

*For God has not given us
the spirit of fear;
but of power,
and of love,
and of a sound mind.*

2 Timothy 1:7 KJV2000

4

Accusation Stinks!

Noble Doss made just one mistake. He dropped the ball. Once. In 1941, he let the ball slip through his fingers. It haunted him the rest of his life. His one mistake cost the team the national championship. The *only* thing between Noble and the goal was about fifteen yards of grass. The quarterback threw the ball right to him. Texas Longhorn fans rose to their feet. Noble saw the ball, and then reached out for it, but his timing was a bit off. He said, "I'll think about that play for the rest of my life." And he did.

Fast-forward fifty years, to 1991. Noble met the new Longhorn coach David McWilliams. As Noble told David of that day long ago when his mistake cost the whole team the national championship, tears came to his own eyes. Half a century had passed, and Noble had allowed self-accusation to dominate his thought process for fifty years. One stinkin' thought had created a stronghold over his entire life.

Self-talk has a way of shaping our lives.

"The mistake I made defines me. I find myself guilty. So does everyone else. There is no way forward." *Now that is one serious pile of stinkin' thinkin'!*

How about you? Does one mistake dominate your thought life? Do you feel guilt over personal imperfection? Does an inner voice often accuse you of dropping the ball?

"I'm not good enough." *Stinkin' thinkin'!*

"I'm not smart enough." *Stinkin' thinkin'!*

"I'm not attractive enough." *Stinkin' thinkin'!*

Whoopin' Up on Stinkin' Thinkin'

"I'm not perfect enough." *Stinkin' thinkin'!*

"I'm just not enough." *Stinkin' thinkin'!*

Have you ever stopped long enough to consider the source of accusation's voice? Those who are in a personal relationship with God through faith in Christ have received God's complete forgiveness and live in his grace, which covers all sin. The voice of accusation is not from God.

Since it is self who is accusing self, it would appear that the voice of accusation is indeed coming from self. The truth, however, is that though you may be accusing yourself, you are simply repeating what the accuser himself keeps whispering in your ear. It's just that you've repeated the accusations so long you may have begun to assume that you are the source of the accusations and that the accusations are an accurate valuation of your life.

Satan daily points out your faults and weaknesses, attempting to bring you down. Run to God's grace!

Sometimes, the accusations come from other people, not yourself. How should you respond? Instead of lashing out against the person, discern if there is any truth in what is said, and learn what you can. At the same time realize that Satan uses the accusations of others to bring you down, sometimes more easily than self-accusations. Stop living by the opinions other people have about you.

Zechariah chapter 3 serves as a great case study in just how much accusation stinks. Zechariah is an obscure Old Testament book, very hard to find. There is a way to find it quickly. Use the table of contents. Or just ask Siri.

> The accuser, Satan, was . . .
> making accusations against Jeshua.
> (Zech 3:1)

Zechariah and Haggai lived at a time when God's people had been used and abused for seventy years of exile in Babylon. Finally, they were returning to Jerusalem.

Most everyone who had left Jerusalem seven decades prior had passed away in Babylon. Those returning to Jerusalem found their ancestral homes crumbled into piles of rubble, along with the temple and city walls.

Under Nehemiah's leadership, they worked together to rebuild the wall. They built their own houses, but neglected temple reconstruction for twenty years. Many of them had neglected God the entire time they were in Babylon. The people had become preoccupied with their own problems

Accusation Stinks!

and pursuits. Zechariah and Haggai got them working together to rebuild the temple.

Zechariah was given visions and messages from God. One vision was about God at work in the life of the leader Joshua. This is not the Joshua who fought the battle of Jericho. This Joshua (also spelled *Jeshua*) was high priest. He offered sacrifices on behalf of the people.

Once a year, he alone would enter the holy of holies, but first he would perform purification rites and ceremonial cleansing. When going into the holy of holies, he wore a bell so people would know he was still alive. A rope was tied to him so that if the bell quit ringing, they could pull him out, since the presence of God in the place was so powerful he might die. This high priest Joshua is the accused in Zechariah chapter 3.

Imagine the scene. You are sitting in a courtroom observing a trial. The judge is sitting in the judgment seat, looking the courtroom over. He is the Father God, intent on bringing true justice. The prosecuting attorney is pacing back and forth, looking over the accused from all angles. He is Satan, laser focused on bringing to light all the faults of the accused, and slanting every detail of the accused's life toward guilt.

> *Satan, the prosecuting attorney, says you are guilty. God the Father is the judge, who gives you the verdict of not guilty. Which voice are you hearing?*

Jesus, the defense attorney, is there, standing with feet firmly planted, blocking the full attack of the prosecutor's gaze. There at the table, you see the accused. You look carefully. Is it Joshua or is it a mirror reflecting your own image? And is there a crowd of people in the mirror as well, representing all those who belong to God by faith in Christ?

There is such a courtroom each day of your life. Satan points out your every imperfection, attempting to make a guilty verdict on your life. Satan will deliberately put people in your life's path as visual reminders to help him point out all your faults, reinforcing his accusations against you. Here are three keys to dealing with the accuser.

DISCERN WHEN THE ENEMY IS ACCUSING YOU

Zechariah was being given a tour by an angel who was helping Zechariah see things from God's perspective. As a child of God, you are surrounded by angels, available to help you see God's true perspective on your circumstances. Calling all angels!

> Then the angel showed me Jeshua, the high priest
> standing before the angel of the Lord.
> The Accuser, Satan, was there at the angel's right hand,
> making accusation against Jeshua.
> (Zech 3:1)

The devil's name is not just a meaningless word. By definition, the word *sadan* (Satan) means the accuser, the one who condemns, the one who opposes. The accuser challenges our worth as God's people. He questions the sincerity of our walk with God. He works through people, both from within God's family and without, to bring us down.

The accuser uses lies to immobilize us. He says things like, "Joshua, you've just come from Babylon. You are a newbie here. What do you know?" He will often give us a one-two punch. He will lure us into temptation by saying, "It will be so enjoyable. Everyone is doing it!" Then once we have given in to temptation, he will say, "How could you have been so stupid! You stooped to doing something that bad? And you call yourself a follower of Christ? I wouldn't know it by looking at you! Shame! Shame! Shame!" Before long, you start agreeing with his accusations, and repeating them to yourself.

"I'm guilty of so many things, it's shameful." *Stinkin' thinkin'!*
"I'm not important." *Stinkin' thinkin'!*
"I don't measure up." *Stinkin' thinkin'!*
"My life hasn't amounted to much." *Stinkin' thinkin'!*
"I'm just a sinner." *Stinkin' thinkin'!*

Many of us live our lives with deep-seated self-deprecation. Satan's accusing voice never seems to let up. We become convinced that everyone agrees with that voice we hear inside our heads. We sing along with Linda Ronstadt, "You're no good. You're no good. You're no good. Baby, you're no good."

Guilt is real. We are all guilty of sin before God. Our verdict before God actually *is* guilty. However, Jesus served our sentence for us on the cross. Those who have come to him for forgiveness are no longer guilty. There is no condemnation for those who are in Christ (Rom 8:1)!

If you are in Christ, then you are not just a sinner! You have become a new creation in Christ Jesus empowered by the indwelling Spirit of Christ to live a life fully able to serve God and others. For those in Christ, the Holy Spirit within convicts us of sin, so that by confessing our sin, fellowship with God is restored. This is entirely different than Satan's accusations, which tend to beat us down and destroy our fellowship with God.

Step one in dealing with the accuser is discerning when he is accusing you. How can we discern between the accusation of Satan and the conviction of the Holy Spirit? Paul wrote a letter to help convict the believers in Corinth of sin in their lives.

> I am not sorry that I sent that severe letter to you,
> ... I know it was painful to you for a little while.
> ... the pain caused you to repent
> and change your ways.
> It was the kind of sorrow God wants his people to have,
> ... the kind of sorrow God wants us to experience
> leads us away from sin and results in salvation.
> There's no regret for that kind of sorrow.
> But worldly sorrow, which lacks repentance,
> results in spiritual death.
> (2 Cor 7:9–10 NLT)

Accusation comes from Satan and, like conviction, brings sorrow over sin. However, unlike conviction, the accusation of Satan seeks to put you in bondage and pull you away from God. Accusation makes you feel guilty, worthless, and stupid, all of which increases your sorrow without pointing out to you the possibility of repentance and restoration.

The conviction of the Holy Spirit also produces sorrow over sin, yet does so to cause confession and repentance. Once you agree with God about your sin, you are able to turn from it, asking and readily receiving his forgiveness and overflowing grace. Sorrow vanishes. Joy, peace, and confidence in Christ become rooted in who you are.

> *Learn to discern between Satan's accusation and the Spirit's conviction.*

How can you know which sorrow you are experiencing? Here is the key issue: Is regret over sin keeping you away from God? If so, you are listening to the enemy's voice of accusation, not the Spirit's voice of conviction. Draw near to God. Resist the devil, and he will flee from you (Jas 4:7).

Remember, Satan is *not* your judge! He is merely the prosecuting attorney. Don't let his accusations intimidate you! He may tell you that the bad things happening in your life are punishment. He may tell you that you are serving a sentence for all the bad you have done. Karma is your king. *Stinkin' thinkin'!*

Yes, it is true that you reap what you sow, but God's grace and forgiveness trumps everything!

Discerning Satan's accusation has not come easy for me. I've paid a high price for an accusation education, and it seems I am still enrolled in that University of Hard Knocks!

While sharing the gospel in a communist country, we were accused of being government spies, illegally smuggling people out of the country, holding anti-patriotic meetings, and spreading spiritual pollution. Though dealing with those accusations was not easy, the spiritual harvest we were gathering for the kingdom made the accusations bearable.

Oddly enough, accusation caught me by surprise after returning from overseas, when I began pastoring established, institutionalized churches. I had started new churches and pastored them before going overseas, but never had I encountered anything quite like the 80 percent of established churches in the United States which are experiencing decline.

My education at the University of Hard Knocks has taught me many reasons why our churches are in decline. Though the vast majority of people in these churches have been absolutely supportive and a joy to serve, it seems that most every declining church has a power base of two or three people who, though not in official positions of authority, wield invisible control over virtually everything. These power people enjoy retaining power for themselves, sometimes even by accusing and running off their pastors.

I have been accused of not visiting the hospital, yet no name could be given of someone in the hospital whom I had not visited. I have been accused of training people to share their faith without first getting the approval of the church. (Guilty as charged.) An accusation even came that I was trying to get the church to be more involved in missions. (Guilty there, as well!)

One man who never came to worship after my first sermon accused me of preaching sermons that bored him! If passionate, practical, biblical sermons don't light someone's fire, the person's wood is just too wet!

I could easily allow these accusations to pull me down into the stinkin' thinkin' of beating up on myself emotionally. I could easily believe that I am not a worthwhile person, that God hasn't really called me into the ministry, that I don't have what it takes to be a good pastor, that everyone is out to get me, that I am not a likeable person, blah, blah, blah. I must not let myself become identified by what accusers say about me. I must be on guard against stinkin' thinkin', and must find my true identity in how God feels about me.

If I am not careful however, my reaction to these accusations won't only pull me down into negative emotions. My reaction may also lift me up into stinkin' prideful thinkin'. I could easily start thinking the accusers are all wrong and I am right all the time on every issue. I could pride myself with a martyr's complex, thinking I alone am the spiritual one, and unspiritual people are out to get me because I am so spiritual.

> *Whoopin' up on stinkin' thinkin' requires self-talk on who you are and whose you are.*

Professional athletes talk to themselves. I once had a friend who spent four years of doctoral study examining the self-talk of athletes. Self-talk can have some benefit, *if* we recognize it, evaluate it, and most of all let God in on the conversation.

Are you examining your self-talk? Whoopin' up on stinkin' thinkin' involves changing our self-talk.

Are you suffering under the accuser's attack? Here is some needed self-talk for the child of God in Christ. This is your true identity:

I am God's child.
I am seen by God just like he sees his own son Jesus.
I am rescued from the judgment fire of Satan.
I stand before God fully and deeply loved.
I am God's precious one.
I am accepted in totality just as I am.
Satan may accuse me, but he is a big, fat liar.

Say each one of those lines aloud while looking in a mirror. Repeat each line five times before going to the next line. Post the words where you can see them often. Tell a trusted brother or sister in Christ who you are in Christ. Ask them to remind you who you are in Christ. Do the same for them.

Here's the second step in dealing with the accuser.

Whoopin' Up on Stinkin' Thinkin'

OVERCOME ACCUSATION THROUGH GOD'S GRACE

When Satan accuses you, take the accusation to God. It's best to let God deal with the accuser on your behalf, instead of talking it out with Satan directly. Satan is more scared of God than he is of you. Don't open up a dialogue with Satan. God is the one who has allowed Satan to hold court on you. He has a purpose in it that *he* will work out. Let him do so.

The accuser says, "You are guilty, and deserve the eternal fires of hell." God says in Christ . . .

You Are Cleared of All Charges

> And the Lord said to Satan,
> "I, the Lord, reject your accusations, Satan.
> Yes, the Lord, who has chosen Jerusalem, rebukes you.
> This man is like a burning stick
> that has been snatched from the fire."
> (Zech 3:2)

You have judicial clearance from the Judge himself. He has declared you innocent. Through Christ, you have been plucked from the fires of eternal damnation. Satan cannot make his charges against you stick, because he is sick in the head, and because Jesus Christ has justified you. No weapon formed against you will stand (Isa 54:17).

Who dares accuse you when God has chosen you for his own? No one! God himself has given you right standing before him. Who will condemn you? No one! For Christ Jesus died for you and nothing can separate you from his love (Rom 8:33–35).

The accuser says, "You are filthy. There's no way to clean you up, you good-for-nothing scum bag." God says that in Christ . . .

You Are Clean of All Filth

> Jeshua's clothing was filthy
> as he stood there before the angel.
> So the angel said to the others standing there,
> "Take off his filthy clothes."

Accusation Stinks!

> And turning to Jeshua he said,
> "See, I have taken away your sins,
> and now I am giving you these fine new clothes."
> (Zech 3:3–4 NLT)

When you place your life into the hands of Christ, asking his forgiveness of your sin and surrendering the control over your life to him, you change positions. Previously, you were in a position of guilt because of rebellion against God. Your clothes were dirty. But when you turned away from self-centered living and turned to Christ, you moved into a new position. Your standing with God is that of full acceptance. Your clothes are fresh and clean. You are justified!

When I need a reminder, I just ask the angels around me, "How are my spiritual clothes looking these days, guys?"

"Mighty fine, Matthew, mighty fine. We've got your back. We've got your front. We've got your left and your right. We're below you and above you. Work with us, and we'll keep you clean. We've got this!"

Before Christ entered your life, you were God's creation, yet you were covered in the filth of sin. Once Christ came into your life, you became God's child.

At the point of repentance and faith in Christ, he changes your clothes. He takes off your sinful rags and clothes you in white linen. His angel attendants give you a fine new wardrobe.

Are you still dressed in the filthy rags of sin, or have you become clothed in Christ? How is your wardrobe? Is your dirty laundry piling up, or are you washed in the blood of the Lamb?

H. A. Ironside, pastor of Moody Church of Chicago, once said, "God will discipline his failing people, but he will not allow Satan to place a charge against us, for provision has been made for us to come into his presence through Christ."

The accuser says, "You are one nappy-headed fellow. I've never seen the likes of you before, all crowned in dandruff and what not." God says that in Christ . . .

You Are Crowned in Honor

> Then I said, "They should also place a
> clean turban on his head."

> So they put a clean priestly turban on his head
> and dressed him in new clothes
> while the angel of the LORD stood by.
> (Zech 3:5)

None of this is a do-it-yourself project. God does the clearing of all charges. There is no plea bargaining. God cleans away all filth. There is no shower you can take to wash away your sin. God does the crowning in honor. There's no store that sells priestly turbans. Only God has them. He gives all of this freely as undeserved gifts to those who repent and turn to Christ. That's what grace is and does.

> *Grace is God giving undeserved gifts to those who repent and turn to Christ.*

In the Middle East, a man is identified by his turban. When you think of the new turban being wrapped around Joshua's head, picture God's renewal of your mind. He is wrapping his thoughts around your brain. He is protecting your mind from accusation by surrounding you with his truth. Your new turban identifies you as belonging to Christ.

It was Zechariah who suggested to God that Joshua get a new turban. Who do you know who might need a new turban? You can bring their need for a renewed mind before the Lord. Who is on your heart? What joy will be yours when you see God respond to your prayer, and you watch as he wraps the turban of renewal around your friend's mind.

Satan, the accuser, says, "You are useless to God. Why would you even think of offering yourself to him? Don't insult him by doing so!" However, God says that in Christ . . .

You Are Commissioned to Serve

> Then the angel of the LORD spoke very solemnly
> to Jeshua and said, "This is what
> the LORD of Heaven's Armies says:
> 'If you follow my ways and carefully serve me,
> then you will be given authority over my Temple
> and its courtyards. I will let you walk
> among these others standing here.'"
> (Zech 3:6–7)

As God's people, we have been given the authority of Christ to be his ambassadors to the world (Matt 28:18–20). We share in his authority. Satan does not want you to realize that truth, and he certainly doesn't want you living a witnessing lifestyle in the power of Christ's authority. Those in Christ are empowered to stand as go-betweens, connecting people to God, and God to people.

As Christ followers, we are privileged to walk among the finest people on the planet; God's people. We enjoy fellowship among God's cleared, cleaned, crowned, and commissioned people. There is, however, a condition.

The condition has to do with your ability to live out your faith. The condition is that in order to fully live out your commission, you must follow the ways of the Lord and serve him wholeheartedly. The condition does not involve your standing with the Lord. Your standing with God is unconditional. Your position in Christ is permanent and irreversible.

To the degree that you crucify the flesh daily and walk in the Spirit, you will enjoy the fulfillment of the commission God gives you. Remember, God promised Joshua that "if you follow my ways and carefully serve me, then you will be given authority over my Temple and its courtyards" (Zech 3:7).

You must see yourself as dead to sin and alive to God. Take every thought captive and make them obey Christ. You will then be able to fulfill the plan God has for your life. You will have his power and influence to lead in meaningful, spiritual worship. Every *secular* space you invade will become a *sacred* place of spiritual discussion as God's courtyard.

God's grace clears our minds of guilt. God's grace cleans our bodies from filth. God's grace crowns our thought life with the honor we share with Christ as part of God's royal family. By God's grace we have the undeserved favor placed on us of being commissioned to serve as his global representatives. Overcome the accusations of Satan with God's overflowing grace.

Time for some needed self-talk:
"In Christ Jesus . . .
I am cleared of all charges.
I am clean of all filth.
I am crowned in honor.
I am commissioned to serve.
I meet his condition: I obey with all my heart."

REMEMBER CHRIST TRUMPS THE ACCUSER

As a book of prophecy, Zechariah speaks on behalf of God on multiple levels; the present, the near future, and the ultimate future.

> Listen to me, O Jeshua the high priest, and all other priests.
> You are symbols of things to come.
> (Zech 3:8a NLT)

The things to come are plural, referring, it seems, to three things. The first fulfillment of this prophecy occurred when Zerubbabel led the Jews out of captivity in Babylon and rebuilt the temple. Worship was restored in Jerusalem during Zechariah's lifetime. The Jews of Jerusalem, after the rebuilding of Jerusalem, experienced a time of revival and peace as a nation.

> *God says, "I have a solution for the accusations you face: Jesus!"*

The second fulfillment of this prophecy occurred at the coming of Christ, which happened about five hundred years after Zechariah's time. It is amazing that the Old Testament so often points to Jesus!

> Soon I am going to bring my servant, the Branch.
> (Zech 3:8b)

Isaiah had prophesied (Isa 11:1) that a branch would spring up from the root of Jesse, David's father. Jesus came from the lineage of David. God came to the earth himself, being born as the man Jesus, who was both 100 percent man and 100 percent God at the same time.

In response to Satan's accusation, God says, "I have a solution for the enemy's attempts at condemning people. The solution I am sending is Jesus."

God says, "Here I am in the person of Jesus. Jesus is me, myself, and I. Though the accuser comes to destroy, I come to this earth to whoop up on Satan's stinkin' accusation thinkin' and give you life."

> "Now look at the jewel I have set before Jeshua,
> a single stone with seven facets.

> I will engrave an inscription on it,"
> says the Lord of Heaven's Armies,
> "and I will remove the sins of this land
> in a single day."
> (Zech 3:9 NLT)

The stone mentioned is a capstone, which is the wedge stone at the top of an arch. It is the crown of the building. The word *facet* may best be translated as "eye." Now picture that capstone having seven sides to it, each side with an eye. Such is the perfect vision and judgment of Christ.

On Christ's cross, in the capstone position, was engraved the designation "King of the Jews." In one single day on the cross, Jesus removed the sins of all who turn to him by faith. He is King of kings, and Lord of lords.

The third aspect of Zechariah's prophecy is the return of Christ, which will be fulfilled in the future. When Christ returns, in one single day he will cause mass numbers of Jews to believe in him. Just as Zechariah and many Old Testament prophets prophesied, Jerusalem will be restored as the holy land, her sins forgiven, and her land healed. Christ will return with the names of all Israel engraved on the stones of his breastplate. When Christ returns, there will be peace in Jerusalem.

> *Victorious living, even in the middle of the worst accusations, is within reach now, through Christ.*

> "And on that day,"
> says the Lord of Heaven's Armies,
> "each of you will invite your neighbor
> to sit with you peacefully
> under your own grapevine and fig tree."
> (Zech 3:10)

Just before the return of Christ, the world will tribulate for seven years. The accuser will slander and accuse God's person, God's place, and God's people (Rev 13:6) However, after the thousand-year reign of Christ on earth, the accuser will be thrown into the fires of hell to be tormented forever (Rev 20:7–10)!

Satan, for now, is given permission by God to accuse us, but there is a day coming when Christ will ultimately triumph over the accuser. For

Whoopin' Up on Stinkin' Thinkin'

God's people, victorious living is within reach even now, even in the midst of the accuser's most vicious attacks, as we discern when the enemy is accusing us, overcome accusation through God's grace, and remember that Christ trumps the accuser.

In Stanford, California, during the 1970s, an ad was placed in the paper asking for volunteers for an unusual experiment that is still discussed today. What would it be like to be falsely accused and put in prison? To answer that question, a fake prison was set up at Stanford University, and half of the volunteers were trained to be accusatory guards. The other half played the role of prisoners.

The "guards" dressed the part, went to the homes of the "prisoners," arrested them, dressed them in prison uniforms, placed them in their cells, and began humiliating them with accusation. Though the experiment was designed to last several weeks, it was halted after less than one week. While many or most of the guards seemed to enjoy their role, many of those being accused became depressed, angry, and anxious, and had to be taken out of the experiment. The director of the experiment had to remind the accused that they were *not* prisoners.

People who are repeatedly accused easily become falsely imprisoned by the resulting emotions. Satan is the real accuser who lies to us, trying to make us think his make-believe prison is real.

The accuser tells us we are guilty, when the truth is there is no condemnation for those in Christ (Rom 8:1). Satan says we are imprisoned by sin, yet the truth is we are no longer slaves to sin (Rom 6:6). He accuses us of being filthy, however we are actually clothed in righteousness (1 Cor 1:30). Satan shows us fake prison walls, while Christ has set us free (Gal 5:1).

ACCUSATION STINKS!

Questions for Reflection and Discussion

Do specific mistakes dominate your thought life? What are they?

Read Zechariah 3:1–2. Recall the description of the court proceeding in the previous chapter of this book. Imagine taking your mistake to that courtroom in your mind and let the court proceed according to God's truth. Write the verdict here:

Does an inner voice accuse you? Think up a game plan for when you hear the voice. What is your predetermined plan of action?

Read Zechariah 3:3–7. What most impresses you about God's treatment of Joshua?

Read Zechariah 3:8–10. Notice how God gets Zechariah's attention along with his kingdom co-laborers. How might God be speaking to you and those on your ministry team? "Listen up, you and your co-laborers in Christ. Here is what I am going to do next." What might God be trying to say to you and your team? What does he have for you next?

Why do you suppose God allows Satan to accuse us?

From this passage, what do you find encouraging about the ministry of angels?

For Scripture exploration, memory, and sharing with others:
2 Corinthians 7:9–10

Romans 8:33–34

Revelation 12:10–11

*Don't be selfish;
don't try to impress others.
Be humble,
thinking of others as
better than yourselves.
Don't look out only for
your own interests,
but take an interest in others, too.*

Philippians 2:3–4 NLT

*Let the gentle wind of God's presence be a magnet
pulling you out of the cave of discouragement.*

5

Discouragement Stinks!

Do you ever wish that your life would end soon? Are you so tired of life that you question why you were born? Does it feel like life has nothing more to offer you? Are you looking around to head to life's nearest exit? If any of these things are true for you, don't despair. You are actually in good company. Some of the greatest heroes of the Bible felt such severe discouragement, as well.

Search Scripture, and you will find that Moses was so overwhelmed with trying to care for the wilderness whiners, he said, "Just kill me now, God!" (Num 11:13-15). Job, so upbeat for so long despite one tragedy after another, finally said, "It would have been better for me never to have been born, God!" (Job 3:11).

> *Some of the greatest heroes of the Bible felt severe discouragement*

Jonah told an entire city of people that God would strike them dead. When God didn't pour out his wrath on the city, Jonah said, "I wish *I* were dead" (Jonah 4:5-11). The great Apostle Paul sometimes felt crushed and overwhelmed, and he despaired of life itself (2 Cor 1:8).

The stink of discouragement lingers on and on, like spray from a skunk. You can't complain discouragement away. You can't drink it away. You can't play it away. You can't just laugh it off. Try to outrun it, and you'll fail.

Whoopin' Up on Stinkin' Thinkin'

Discouragement makes you do strange things. Ask Elijah. After a great victory, discouragement hit Elijah hard, and he ran off and hid in a cave. Can you identify with Elijah? Sometimes, just when most people would assume you are happy about how well things are going for you, do you just want to run away and hide?

In Elijah's discouragement I actually find encouragement. If he, as one of God's bravest and best servants, was struck with discouragement to the point of asking God to let his life end, then I don't feel so bad after all.

Elijah stands as one of the greatest prophets and leaders of the Old Testament. His name is composed of two parts: *El*, which is short for *Elohim* or "God," and *Yah*, which is short for *Yahweh*. *Yahweh* is a common Old Testament name for Jehovah God. Even Elijah's name speaks for God.

Elijah grew up in Tisbeh, a backwoods, rugged place. He was no doubt a leathery sort of man from his teenage days. We see an impressive toughness in his leadership, not unlike a marine drill sergeant.

Notice clearly his style of ministry. As a bold prophet, Elijah directly confronted those who were out of God's will. Completely unafraid of speaking forth the truth of God, he let the word of God land as it would. Elijah even got in the king's face without any hesitation.

Elijah had become a fugitive, hiding out for years. Suddenly, he would appear out of nowhere, pronouncing God's judgment against those who worshipped Baal, then he would disappear again. King Ahab put out an APB on Elijah. Elijah had been on the most most-wanted list for some time.

One day near the broken down altar where people of the past had worshipped the one true God on Mount Carmel, a crowd gathered to worship Baal. The ceremony was complete with 450 prophets of Baal. True to form, out of nowhere came Elijah, standing alone at the altar to the one true God. "If Baal is God, let him light his altar with fire. But if Yahweh is God, then let him light the fire at this altar of the One true God. Choose this day who you will serve."

The Baal worshippers shouted, but no fire fell. They danced, yet still no fire. They even began cutting themselves, however there was no fire at all. Elijah mocked them, saying, "Where is Baal? In the bathroom maybe?"

Elijah poured water over Yahweh's altar, dousing it three times. Then he prayed, "Lord, prove that you are God." Fire fell from heaven! The fire burned up the sacrificial bull and licked up all the water around the altar. What a victory!

DISCOURAGEMENT STINKS!

However, a short time later, the big battle was a distant memory for Elijah. Elijah, the great prophet, developed a disturbed state of mind. With discouragement bordering on suicide, Elijah had a breakdown. He crashed and burned.

Mark it down: after a great victory, the enemy will often attack with stinkin' thinkin'. As a pastor, I can clearly recall seasons of great spiritual advance in the church, only to see a short time later a group within the church develop a stinkin' thinkin' club that seemingly erased all the blessings of the recent victory.

Eight or ten young families join the aging church, bringing in young children and new life. For a short time, the more established members are very happy, but soon they scold the children for acting childlike in the worship center. They question the more free emotional expression of these new young adults during worship. More than anything, there is grief over loss of control. *Whose church has it become now?*

Right after God does a great work, we often allow the enemy to lure us into stinkin' thinkin', which gets us grumbling and distracts us from celebrating.

Let's look at the factors which led to Elijah's discouragement. What specific thoughts brought him to a place of despair?

> *After a great victory, the enemy will attack with stinkin' thinkin'.*

STINKIN' DISCOURAGEMENT THINKIN'

"I Must Fear Powerful People"

Though Elijah had single-handedly confronted King Ahab and 450 prophets of Baal on Mt. Carmel, one particular woman caused him to tuck tail and run; Ahab's wife Jezebel.

> When Ahab got home, he told Jezebel
> everything Elijah had done, including the way
> he had killed all the prophets of Baal.
> So Jezebel sent this message to Elijah:
> "May the gods strike me and even kill me
> if by this time tomorrow I have not killed you
> just as you killed them."
> Elijah was afraid.

Whoopin' Up on Stinkin' Thinkin'

(1 Kgs 19:1–3a)

Four hundred fifty men had not put fear in rugged Elijah. The king himself had not deterred him. Now Jezebel appears, and Elijah runs like a mouse hiding from a cat. Why such fear over one little lady?

Jezebel was the *real* power of the throne. Her husband was a puppet and she was the puppet master. Every move he made was initiated by a string tied to one of her fingers. Through Ahab, she had initiated Baal worship in Israel, and led God's people the farthest away from God they had ever been. She was a master manipulator. It's not surprising that few people these days name a daughter "Jezebel."

Have you ever felt threatened by a powerful person? I know I sure have. As a peacemaker at heart, I want everyone to be happy. For some reason, if a bully shows up and tells me to jump, instead of standing my ground and not being intimidated, my first thought is to ask them how high they want me to jump! *Stinkin' thinkin', Matthew!*

Elijah stood at a place originally dedicated to the worship of the One true God, and most of those who heard his voice had once claimed to serve the Lord. However, their hearts had turned away from him to serve other things.

We live in a day of American idols all across the landscape. Idolatry has even crept in among God's people today. If you boldly call people to choose this day whom they will serve, you will become a target.

My heart is heavy these days for modern day Elijahs. Here's my prayer these days for myself and others who boldly speak for God: "Lord, as we speak your unpopular truth, there are many who simply don't want to hear it. They would silence our voices, one way or another. Father, remove our fear. Help us defy our inhibition and walk like lions across this land. By your Spirit, we are bold. With every step we take, we walk victorious into places in which you have already gone before us."[1]

> When you are discouraged, where do you run? Run to God.

Whatever the conflict, nearly all of us at one time or another have been threatened by a Jezebel. Though she may have no official title or credentials, everyone knows she is the boss. When you feel threatened, consider the source. If a godly person speaks to you, you should

---

1. See YouTube: "Lions," by Skillet

listen carefully. However, the Jezebel in your life is *not* a godly person. He or she is not being led by God. Fear God, but do *not* fear carnal people.

In God's eyes, a powerful CEO and a homeless person are both of equally great value. Why should you fear someone who is, according to God, of equal value to you?

Powerful people are powerful because we give them power. We watch them manipulate people toward their purposes, and we do not confront them. We should instead refuse to tolerate manipulative bullying among God's family. Tell bullies that what they are doing is wrong. If that doesn't work, take a key church leader back with you. If there is still no change, take it before the church (Matt 18:15–17).

I must fear powerful people! Stinkin' thinkin'.

When you are kicked to the curb by a carnal person, instead of reacting in fear, it's time for self-talk and God-talk!

Self-talk: "Listen up, self! Jezebel is not the sovereign one. God is in control. Don't worry about his or her threats."

God-talk: "God, I will trust in you now just like I have in the past. I will *not* run and hide from bullies or from life."

Here is a second aspect of stinkin' discouragement thinkin'.

"I Must Run from My Problems"

> Elijah was afraid and fled for his life.
> He went to Beersheba, a town in Judah,
> and he left his servant there.
> (1 Kgs 19:3)

Elijah fled from Ahab's area of domain, and as he crossed over into the territory of Judah, he no doubt breathed a sigh of relief. Running away causes you to feel that you have distanced yourself from the threat of powerful people. However, running from bullies doesn't cause them to go away!

When you are discouraged, do you run to distract yourself? Where do you run? Do you run to a bottle? Do you run to a recreational place? Do you find yourself in a comedy club? Do you run to temptation? Do you run to mama?

I must run from my problems! Stinkin' thinkin'!

Needed self-talk: "When discouraged by those who enjoy wielding power over me, I will run only to God! I will not run away from my problems."

God-talk: "Here I am with all my inhibitions, Lord. It's a big world out there and some people are out to bring me down. By your Spirit, make me bold and wise."

"It's Better to Be Alone"

> Then he went on alone into the wilderness,
> traveling all day.
> He sat down under a solitary broom tree . . .
> (1 Kgs 19:4a)

When discouraged, the *last* thing we need is to be alone! Like a dying animal, we are prone to go off by ourselves and bear the pain in solitude. When we are discouraged, we think no one else understands us, so we distance ourselves from others. Discouraged people are lonely people. Discouraged people go out into their own little wilderness and pout under a tree.

"A juniper (broom) tree is small. There's only room for one under its barren branches of discouragement and loneliness. There is little shade."[2]

> *Maybe discouragement has been your best friend for a long time. Time for new friends!*

It's better to be alone. Stinkin' thinkin'.

Self-talk: "I'm discouraged. I'll go spend a couple of days with an encouraging friend."

God-talk: "Lord, I don't want a pity party under a juniper tree. I want to be refreshed by you and by your people. Make yourself known to me. Take me to life-giving people of grace."

"It's Better to Die"

> He sat down under a solitary broom tree
> and prayed that he might die.
> "I've had enough, Lord," he said. "Take my life . . ."

2. Charles Swindoll, "Insight for Living" Broadcast

(1 Kgs 19:4)

In the original Hebrew, Elijah's prayer is short and to the point, consisting of only four words: "Enough, Lord. Take me." Maybe you've lived off the adrenaline of exciting events and now you just want to crash. Or maybe discouragement has been your best friend for a long time, so long that you are ready for life to end.

It's better to die. Stinkin' thinkin'.

Self-talk: "Am I thinking straight? No! Come on self. Snap out of it. Life is good because God is good! Look for the good. Look for God. He wants to be found."

God-talk: "God, life is hard. Strengthen me. Give me a renewed will to live. Remove my self-absorption. Captivate my heart with you."

"I Don't Measure Up"

> Take my life, for I am no better
> than my ancestors . . .
> (1 Kgs 19:4)

We are so prone to compare ourselves with others, and come out short. Don't you wish you could have been eavesdropping on Elijah as he sat under that solitary tree? If I would have been within earshot of him, I would have approached him and said, "Elijah, whoever said you had to be better than your grandpa or your dad?"

Is your discouragement brought on in part because you have placed unrealistic expectations on yourself? Are you performance driven? Does your sense of worth come from achievement? Are you competitive, unable to relax until you have proven your worth by your accomplishments?

I don't measure up. Stinkin' thinkin'.

Self-talk: "Why does it always have to be about me anyway? I'm tired of striving. I turn to God for my sense of worth."

> *Stinkin' thinkin' keeps the heart from experiencing God.*

God-talk: "God, instead of me setting the standards, I leave that to you, since that's really your job anyway. I am so glad that you have given me your grace through my faith in Christ. You are loving, accepting, and affirming. When stinkin' thinkin' attacks me, I run to your grace."

Whoopin' Up on Stinkin' Thinkin'

"No One Even Cares about Me or about God"

> Then he lay down and slept . . .
> But as he was sleeping, an angel touched him
> and told him, "Get up and eat!"
> He looked around and there beside his head
> was some bread baked and hot stones
> and a jar of water! . . . So he got up and ate and drank,
> and the food gave him enough strength
> to travel forty days and forty nights to Mount Sinai,
> the mountain of God. There he came to a cave,
> where he spent the night. But the Lord said to him,
> "What are you doing here, Elijah?"
> Elijah replied,
> "I have zealously served the Lord God Almighty.
> But the people of Israel have broken their covenant
> with you, torn down your altars,
> and killed every one of your prophets.
> I am the only one left,
> and now they are trying to kill me too."
> (1 Kgs 19:5–10)

The goodness and patience of God is shown to Elijah. The Lord gave him the touch of an angel, who cooked and catered a hot meal for Elijah. God allowed Elijah time to rest and refresh.

Had you and I been the Lord dealing with Elijah, we might have said, "Suck it up, Elijah! Get up! Get back on the job!"

However, God is a loving Father, slow to rebuke us. He is not prone to blame us. He does not want to shame us. There was no quick correction of Elijah's stinkin' thinkin'. Instead, God said, "Take it easy, my child. Rest. Eat. Rest some more. Eat some more. We can talk when you are ready."

After Elijah was refreshed by an angel, he journeyed to Sinai. Elijah knew Sinai to be a place where God had revealed his glory. Perhaps he was going there to seek God. However, a journey that should have taken only four or five days took Elijah forty days. It seems he was wandering aimlessly, lost in discouragement. When he finally arrived at Sinai, he hid in a cave.

On seeing a cave, Elijah might have said to himself, "A cave! Inside a dark cavern is a better place for a pity party than under a tree!" Though

Elijah is at Mount Sinai, geographically at a great place for experiencing God, his heart is not at such a place yet. It's funny how a person can be at exactly that right place where others have had life-changing encounters with Christ, yet not be transformed. Stinkin' thinkin' keeps the heart from being in the right place to experience God.

Though Elijah received the refreshment God provided his body, he was not yet looking for God to restore and refresh his soul. No, Elijah wanted to be bitter for a while longer. He was not done being frazzled and discouraged. When God speaks to him, Elijah, full of pity, replies, "I've been serving you all by myself all this time, and what do I get? The lonely life of a fugitive!"

Elijah assumed that he was the only one who cared about God. When I have been attacked by carnal people, I find it tempting to assume that very thing; that I am the only person walking with God. If that sounds prideful, it is. It's time to look around for other godly people. They can be found, if sought out.

Elijah also assumed that no one cared about him. Why did he assume such? Because no human being had ministered to him in any practical way. Why had no human done so? Because Elijah had withdrawn himself from all human contact! When you get discouraged and build emotional walls around yourself, no one even has a chance to care about you!

At a church I pastored, there were many, many wonderful people. However, there was one particular deacon who, for some reason, led a year-long campaign against me, saying repeatedly in church gatherings, "We have to make our pastor bleed." He always held out the vowel sound as he said, "bleeeeeed."

For a short time, some listened to him, but over time, he lost his power. I will not fear carnal people of supposed power. I refuse to retaliate. I will not develop a martyr complex and crawl in a hole all alone. I choose instead to consider opposition as a normal part of serving God, and depend heavily on God and godly people for protection, strength, and sanity.

Self-talk: "I'm in a cave because of my own stinkin' thinkin'. There's a beautiful mountain outside this cave. If I get out of this dark place and go out there, I might just experience God. There might even be some of God's people out there as well."

God-talk: "Lord, I've been restless. I've kept myself in the dark. I come out to you in the light of day. Restore my soul as only you can. Help me to discern who I can trust with my soul. Bring me into heart-to-heart relationships with others who genuinely love you."

Before we move on to what God seeks to do for us when we are discouraged, let's review the stinkin' thinkin' behind discouragement:

- "I must fear powerful people."
- "I must run from my problems."
- "It's better to be alone."
- "It's better to die."
- "I don't measure up."
- "No one even cares about God or about me."

Are any of these thoughts prevalent in your mind? Which ones? What do you need to tell yourself? What kind of conversation do you need to have with God?

Though there are certainly many other thoughts that might lead to discouragement, our case study of Elijah has pointed toward those thoughts we have just explored. From the same case study, we now examine how God gets involved when we are discouraged.

GOD WHOOPS UP ON ELIJAH'S STINKIN' THINKIN'

When you are discouraged, look for God to make himself more real to you than perhaps ever before. Get ready for him to show up in tangible, powerful ways. God will not let his child stay down forever. God is gracious. When you are tired, he gives you rest. When you are hungry, he gives you food. When you are lonely, he gives you the touch of an angel. When you are confused, he gives you direction. When you are discouraged, he lifts you up.

He Repositions

> There he came to a cave,
> where he spent the night . . .
> and a voice said,
> "What are you doing here Elijah?"

Discouragement Stinks!

(1 Kgs 19:9, 13)

Our way of thinking might put the emphasis on the word *here*. "Elijah, why are you at Mount Sanai in this cave?" However, the original Hebrew puts the emphasis on the word "doing." The original wording was literally, "What *do* you here?"

Our physical location may say more about us than simply revealing our GPS latitude and longitude. We have arrived at a particular location because there is an activity at that location which we feel is worth the effort to get there and the time invested to stay there. What are you doing where you are now? What an important question!

> *Discouraged? Consider what you are doing where you are. Does God want to reposition you?*

If there is no valid answer as to what God-given purpose has brought you to the GPS coordinates where you physically are now in life, then it may very well be that God wants to reposition you, both geographically and cognitively.

Cognitive repositioning? What does that look like? A cognitive reposition is a mental shift. One example would be moving from discouragement to eagerness in accepting God's next adventure for you. His next adventure might move you geographically. Do not let discouragement hinder God's repositioning of you.

Here's how God repositioned Elijah from the cave to a more inspirational place in life.

> Go out and stand before me on the mountain.
> (1 Kgs 19:11)

Are you willing to be repositioned, cognitively? Are you willing for your mind to get out of the rut of stinkin' discouragement? Are you ready to have your thoughts lifted out of the darkness? God is calling you out of the cave.

Two men were in the same room looking out the same window at night. One saw mud. The other saw stars. Which do you see?

God wants you to get out of your cave and stand before him on the mountain. He waits to meet you there at inspiration point. God Almighty himself is speaking directly to you, offering you a personal invitation to meet with him! How much more encouragement could you possibly want? A personal experience with the Lord will lift you up out of discouragement like nothing else! Hear his voice. Stand before him.

Whoopin' Up on Stinkin' Thinkin'

When your mind becomes completely free of self-directed living, you will gladly go to wherever God may reposition you. Perhaps nothing might discourage you more than not being in the physical place God wants you to be. In a world in which there are entire countries where less than two percent of the population has ever even heard the name "Jesus," do you think it is God's will for Christians to remain huddled together in gospel-saturated places like the United States? Are you willing to let God geographically reposition you?

Have you settled for self-directed living instead of experiencing the adventure of God-directed living? Self-directed living puts you in a dark cave. God says to you what he said to Elijah: "What *do* you here?" What are you doing sulking mindlessly in a dark place? Are you where God wants you to be in your thinking process? If so, be encouraged. If not, let him reposition you cognitively.

He Patiently Listens

Stinkin' thinkin' causes us to sit in a cave and rehearse to ourselves our own stinkin' thinkin'! The amazing thing is that God willingly enters our cave of discouragement and actually listens to us replay our misery to him over and over again!

God asked, "What *do* you here, Elijah?"

> Elijah replied, "I have zealously served
> the Lord God Almighty.
> But the people of Israel have broken their covenant
> with you, torn down your altars,
> and killed every one of your prophets.
> I am the only one left,
> and now they are trying to kill me too."
> (1 Kgs 19:10)

After carefully listening to all that Elijah had to say, God revealed his great power to Elijah. However, Elijah continued his stinkin' thinkin'. So again, God asked Elijah, "What *do* you here?"

> He replied again,
> "I have zealously served the Lord God Almighty.
> But the people of Israel have broken their covenant

> with you, torn down your altars,
> and killed every one of your prophets.
> I am the only one left,
> and now they are trying to kill me, too."
> (1 Kgs 19:14)

It's as if Elijah thinks God is deaf, that God was not paying attention, or maybe God was not emotionally sensitive enough to pick up Elijah's feelings the first time around. The most likely reason for Elijah's repetition is simply that discouraged people find it "helpful" to reinforce their negative thoughts by repeating them to others over and over. Doing so "validates" their discouragement.

Some of us have an Elijah-complex. It is heard in our prayers. "God, I just don't know what this world is coming to. Hatred is everywhere. This used to be one nation under you God, but the whole country has gone to pot. No one loves you anymore. Nobody but me. I'm the only one, God."

Yes, God will patiently listen to your bellyaching. It's better to take it to him than to bring it to your pastor! He will lovingly allow you to dump your stinkin' thinkin' on him, repeatedly. He will not, however, allow you to stay in such a stinky place for long.

He Displays His Power

> And as Elijah stood there, the Lord passed by,
> and a mighty windstorm hit the mountain.
> It was such a terrible blast that the rocks were torn loose,
> but the Lord was not in the wind.
> After the wind there was an earthquake,
> but the Lord was not in the earth quake.
> And after the earthquake there was a fire,
> but the Lord was not in the fire.
> And after the fire there was a gentle whisper.
> When Elijah heard it, he wrapped his face in a cloak
> and went out and stood at the entrance of the cave.
> (1 Kgs 19:11–13)

Imagine you are there, and right in front of you, you see wind breaking rocks open, an earthquake splitting the ground in two, and fire falling from heaven. Then you hear a gentle whisper, a sound of soft, stillness. The sound of silence. It is God speaking to you. Let the gentle wind of God's presence be a magnet pulling you out of the cave of discouragement.

God whispers, "Do I have your attention now? Do you remember my great power? Quiet all those noisy inner voices of discouragement so you can hear my whisper."

He Surrounds with Encouraging People

> Then the Lord told him, "Go back the same way
> you came, and travel to the wilderness of Damascus.
> When you arrive there anoint Hazael to be king of Aram.
> Then anoint Jehu son of Nimshi to be king of Israel,
> and anoint Elisha son of Shaphat from the town of
> Abel-meholah to replace you as my prophet.
> Anyone who escapes from Hazael
> will be killed by Elisha!
> Yet I will preserve 7,000 others in Israel
> who have never bowed down to Baal or kissed him!"
> (1 Kgs 19:15–18)

When you are discouraged, ask God to form a victory team around you. Ask him to give you some new assignments. Ask the Lord to give you a close personal friend like Elisha.

God has *not* designed us to live like hermits in caves. He has designed us to live in friendship and community. The church, though not perfect, is where we are drawn together in love and encouragement.

> *God has not designed us to be hermits, but to live in community*

One of the ways I am encouraged the most is by people God has put in my life's path so that I could disciple them as Christ followers. Justin Dennis comes to mind as one such person. Here is his story.

> For many years I suffered from severe anxiety and self-doubt. I was so afraid of failure that I was unwilling to put effort into anything, including my career or my education.
> Overcoming these obstacles to build a successful career and a relationship with a person that I deeply loved took so much pain,

Discouragement Stinks!

sacrifice, and hard work that I believed that I had accomplished this new, happy life by myself.

Looking back at it, I now realize that God was with me through everything but he allowed me to endure the pain and the struggle for his purposes. I am a Jew, however, I did not see God in my life at the time. I believed that God had abandoned me during my struggles and that I had built my new, happy life by myself.

As a result of this, I was a very self-centered person. Pride that I had built a successful career was the most important thing in my life. At the time, there was no place in my life for God.

Late in his life, my father chose to believe in Jesus as the Messiah. Although he had more faith in God than almost anybody that I have ever met, watching him suffer as he died from cancer caused me to become angry and bitter, and I distanced myself from God even more.

I was self-centered and quick to anger, which caused me to lose the woman that I loved. A series of events resulted in my family turning their backs on me. I was also hurt physically and for a time I was unable to do the necessary work to feel successful at my job.

> *What place does God have in your life?*

After all of this happened, I felt as though I was completely alone, and I was in a tremendous amount of pain. I felt as though I would not be able to survive. Out of desperation, I walked into a church and asked for help.

That was the first time that I met Pastor Matthew. Although he had never met me before, as he spoke to me about Jesus, I felt the love of God coming through his words and his heart. A few hours later I accepted Jesus as my savior.

I was unable to realize my stinkin' thinkin' on my own. Pastor Matthew explained to me in a way that I could understand that I had never been alone . . . that God had always been with me and that he had always desired to have a relationship with me.

A few days later I was baptized by Pastor Matthew and from the moment that I walked into the church I was surrounded by people who loved me and who accepted me as part of their church family.

I believe that God did all of this for me. Just as God repositioned Elijah, he repositioned me and changed me from someone who was committed to doing my own will to someone who is committed to doing his will.

Whoopin' Up on Stinkin' Thinkin'

Also like Elijah, God surrounded me with encouraging people who made it possible for me to change. After I accepted Jesus as my Savior, my priorities changed. The business that I had built went from the most important thing in the world to just being a job that I enjoy.

Since then I still struggle at times, but God is with me and he is always working through people like Pastor Matthew to help me to stay on the right path and to do his will.

Now *that* is whoopin' up on discouraging stinkin' thinkin'!

DISCOURAGEMENT STINKS!

Questions for Reflection and Discussion

Read 1 Kings 19:1–9. Ever been surprised by discouragement just after a great victory?

Which of the following thoughts do you find to be recurring in your mind?

__ "I must fear powerful people."
__ "I must run from my problems."
__ "It's better to be alone."
__ "It's better to die."
__ "I don't measure up."
__ "No one even cares about God or about me."

What causes you to think the thoughts marked above?

Read 1 Kings 19:10–14. Is there a part of your life or your thinking where God is trying to get through to you and say, "What *do* you here?"

What will it take for God to get your attention?

Read 1 Kings 19:15–18. In which of the following ways do you need God to whoop up on your stinkin' thinkin'?

____ Reposition me.
____ Patiently listen to me.
____ Display his power to me.
____ Surround me with encouraging people.

If God were to refresh and reposition your life, what would change?

Do you believe those specific changes are possible even now? What will you pray? What will you do? Who will you look to as encouraging people?

> "The weapons we fight with . . .
> have the divine power
> to demolish strongholds."
> (2 Cor 10:4 NIV)
>
> Picture the explosive power of God Almighty
> at work in your thought life!
> The One who has the power to raise the dead
> is changing your thoughts.
> The re-creative power of God Almighty
> is flooding into your mind
> and blasting away strongholds.
>
> God's great gushes of living water
> are washing away all your stinkin' thinkin'
> and replacing it with his truth and light.
> From your inner thoughts outward,
> you are becoming new in Christ.

> Sow a thought,
> and you reap an action.
> Sow an action,
> and you reap a habit.
> Sow a habit,
> and you reap a character.
> Sow a character,
> and you reap a destiny.

*A stronghold is a recurring thought,
which may be partially true and partially false,
designed by the enemy to put your mind in bondage
and destroy your potential
to live the life God has for you.*

*Run to Christ, the bondage breaker! Let him whoop
up on your stinkin' thinkin'!
The mind of Christ can be developed within you, resulting in sanity, serenity, and sound thinking.*

---

*We use our powerful God-tools
for smashing warped philosophies,
tearing down barriers
erected against the truth of God,
fitting every loose thought and emotion and impulse
into the structure of life shaped by Christ.*

*2 Corinthians 10:4–5
The Message Paraphrase*

*If you think you know it all,
You're a fool for sure;
Real survivors
learn wisdom from others.*

*Proverbs 28:26
The Message*

6

Stuck? Rethink for a Change!

You simply must let me tell you about our granddaughter! When "Little Taylor Nance Lady" was two years old, her parents told us on a Saturday that they were arriving to our home the very next day. I immediately started building a tree house for Taylor, which was finished by the time she arrived, despite preaching at church on Sunday morning. Shortest sermon ever!

Every time Taylor Lady comes to our house, she loves to play a game with me. She made up the game, and it is called "Stuck, Baba, stuck." As her "Baba," my part in the game is to help her create situations from which she cannot escape, so that I can rescue her. Now that's my kind of game.

So I grab her by one ankle, turn her upside down, and hoist her up until her foot is on the ceiling and she is hanging upside down by one leg. I then wait for her to say, "Stuck, Baba, stuck." She goes outside and I follow her. She climbs up the tree past the tree house to the point of no return. "Stuck, Baba, stuck." She puts herself in the dog cage, closes the door, latches the latch, and says, "Stuck, Baba, stuck." I snap a picture of Taylor looking very trapped in the dog cage and send it to her mother, who replies, "Baba, what have you done to my daughter?"

Seeing Taylor get stuck is *so* cute! It's fun *pretending* to be stuck. *Actually getting stuck* is entirely different. I remember getting my car stuck in the mud when I was wearing my best clothes. About the only thing worse than that is getting stuck in stinkin' thinkin'. When we get stuck in mental ruts, our lives start to stagnate and stink, and it is *not* cute!

Whoopin' Up on Stinkin' Thinkin'

In the days of westward expansion, wagons followed each other, creating trails, which quickly became deep ruts. About midway across the country, there was a fork in the ruts. Go left, and you would end up in California. Go right, and it would take you to Oregon. A sign in the middle of the fork said, "Choose your ruts carefully. You'll be in them for several hundred miles!"

Choose your thoughts carefully. They determine your life. At the time of this writing, there is a battle going on in the world concerning terrorism. However, there is an even bigger battle going on right now. It is the battle for your mind. It's time to do some whoopin' up on stinkin' thinkin'.

> *Choose your thoughts carefully. They determine your life.*

A missionary led an Indian chief to faith in Christ. Weeks later the missionary visited the chief to see how he was doing. The chief was quiet for some time, and then said, "Two dogs fight inside me."

Baffled, the missionary asked, "Which dog is winning the fight?"

"The one I feed the most."

Your thoughts either feed your flesh or feed your soul. The way you think either keeps you stuck as you are, or allows God to change your life.

Why does one believer experience joy and victory, despite difficult circumstances, while another believer has a bad hair day that ruins everything? The secret is in the way we think.

Why do some believers have more stinkin' thinkin' than others? It is not, as some suppose, a matter of how long a person has been a follower of Christ. It is a matter of how much the believer allows Christ to transform his or her thinking.

Why do some people see amazing change in their lives, while others are frustrated because life never changes? It is not, as some would suppose, simply the "luck of the draw." The secret to amazing change in your life is letting Christ change the way you think.

> Let God transform you
> (Rom 12:2 NLT)

The original Greek word "transform" is *metamorpho*, from which we get our word metamorphosis. In a metamorphosis, something drastically changes forms. A wormy caterpillar is transformed into a beautiful butterfly. A

STUCK? RETHINK FOR A CHANGE!

hopeless man is given an exciting reason to live. A self-centered woman starts genuinely and selflessly caring for others.

Drastic change in your life is possible! Let God transform you. Lasting, impactful metamorphosis of who you are will begin from the inside out. God will cause you to rethink the way you think, and change will be the result. To rethink for a change, five things are required.

RETHINK YOUR BODY

> Give your bodies to God
> because of all he has done for you.
> (Rom 12:1)

"I can do whatever I want with my body. It's mine." *Stinkin' thinkin'*.

"I can give my body to whoever I want, as long as we are both sincere." *Stinkin' thinkin'*.

"I can have an abortion if I want. It's my body." *Stinkin' thinkin'*.

"What I do physically doesn't affect me spiritually." *Stinkin' thinkin'*.

"I can feed my body whatever junk food I want. I can soak my body in alcohol if I want. It makes no difference." *Stinkin' thinkin'*.

Give your body to God.

"My body is weak and wobbly. Would God even want it?" He does.

"My body is young and sleek. Someone's going to get it, alright. But . . . God?" Yes, God!

"My body has B.O. It snores. It has a dirty mind. You don't want it, God!" He does!

"God, my body gets tempted all the time. You'd be embarrassed by my body!" Give him your body.

All religions of the world say, "Clean up your body first, then offer it to deity." God does not say that. He says, "Bring your body to me in its current condition. I want your body."

Following Christ is not *religion*. In religion, you try to make yourself presentable, but you never arrive at a presentable state, because that requires perfection. Following Christ is *relationship*. In relationship, love trumps everything, and perfection is not required.

Here's the needed God-talk: "Lord, here's the body. I have trouble with it. I'm sure you will as well. I give it to you in as-is condition, nonreturnable. I am yours. This body is now your temple. Your Spirit fills this body. Help my body never to grieve your Spirit living within. If I do not please you with my body, let me know quickly."

Christ gave his body for you on the cross. It's only right that you, in return, give him your body. You may spend so much time preserving your body, painting your body, sculpting your body, pouring lotions on your body, and tanning your body that you never get around to giving God your body, and worshipping him by the way you live. Give him your body.

Stuck? Rethink for a change. Rethink your body.

RETHINK WORSHIP

> . . . Give your bodies to God
> because of all he has done for you.
> Let them be a living and holy sacrifice—
> the kind he will find acceptable.
> This is truly the way to worship him.
> (Rom 12:1 NLT)

If you think, "Worship is the Sunday morning compartment of my life," you have another think coming!

If you think, "Worship is something I go to church to do," think again!

If you think, "Worship is about my soul, *not* my lifestyle, my daily habits, or my relationships," then you are doing some stinkin' thinkin'.

It's time to rethink worship. What is worship? Does it begin at eleven o'clock sharp and end at twelve o'clock dull? God is Spirit, and those who worship him must worship him in spirit and in truth (John 4:24).

True worship is your *spirit* responding to God's presence with you all day long every day, and your mind changing to accept God's *truth* as your life's guidance system. *Worship is a lifestyle of spirit-responsiveness to God's truth.*

Let's pause right there: Worship is . . .
a lifestyle
of spirit-responsiveness
to God's truth.

You can walk into a building dedicated to religious activity, sit when everyone sits, stand when everyone stands, sing when everyone sings, close your eyes when everyone closes their eyes, say, "Amen," when everyone says, "Amen," and yet you still have *not* worshipped. While it's true you have been to a worship service, unless your spirit was adjusting itself to God's truth revealed to you during the experience, you have not worshipped.

If after attending such a gathering, you find yourself evaluating the quality of the music, the content and delivery of the message, and the caliber of the people present, then you have made the gathering all about you instead of worshipping. Worship is all about him.

You may be halfway through a very busy tax season as an accountant. You find yourself in a hurry to finish each form and get to the next one, all the while becoming weary. You turn your thoughts to God, and convey to him your feelings and stress. His Spirit impresses on your heart the truth that those who wait on the Lord will have their strength renewed, and will soar high on wings like eagles (Isa 40:31). Your *spirit* is lifted by God's *truth*, and you thank God for his timely truth. You return to your work with his joy and strength in your heart. *That* is worship.

> ... a living and holy sacrifice—
> the kind he will find acceptable.
> This is truly the way to worship him.
> (Rom 12:1)

In the Old Testament days, worship by blood sacrifice was a weekly experience. The people of God chose their very best animal, and took it to the temple. As an act of worship, the blood of the sacrificial animal was shed for the forgiveness of their sins. The blood was sprinkled over the people to symbolize the shed blood covering their sins. Every year at harvest time, the people of God gathered the crops, and gave the first one out of every ten as a sacrificial offering to God in worship. When the writer of Romans talked about sacrifice in worship, the people immediately had images come to mind.

However, here in Romans 12, there is a radically new concept involving sacrifice and worship. The sacrifice given during worship is no longer an animal or the fruit of the land. We are to offer *ourselves* as a sacrifice. The people first hearing this concept must have thought, "What? We give ourselves as sacrifices? How so?"

> *One event changed everything: the cross.*

In their minds, a sacrifice is laid down on the altar, has its blood drained out and sprinkled on people, and then its body is burned. The offering of a human as the sacrifice in worship brought radical thoughts to mind, and correctly so.

Without the shedding of blood, God says there is no forgiveness of sin. The problem with animal sacrifices as a means of atonement is that people sinned, and though they made a sacrifice offering, they went out and sinned again, made a sacrifice offering again, ad nauseam. God said, "I am sick of your sacrifices" (Isa 1:11).

The people were going through religious motions, but they had no desire for their spirits and lives to be molded by God's truth; there was no real worship. It was all religious ritual without personal relationship with God.

One event changed everything: the sacrificial death of Jesus on the cross. Jesus shed his blood once, so that all who would trust in him would be forgiven of all their sin, once for all sin, forever. No more blood sacrifice of animals. That is great news! Our response should be that we give ourselves to Christ as living, holy, acceptable sacrifices.

> *Worship is not worship unless there is sacrifice.*

Worship is not worship unless there is sacrifice. Since worship is the complete giving of yourself to God, the *sacrifice is when you take the parts of you that you are prone to hold back from him, and give them anyway.*

In today's world, a life of obedience to Christ is a costly *sacrifice*. It *will* cost you something.

We are to give him ourselves as *living* sacrifices. We become living sacrifices when we give ourselves fully to God all day long by the way we live.

The offering plate was being passed in church. The boy looked in his pockets. Though he wanted to give, he had nothing to give. So he set the offering plate down on the floor, and stood in the plate. He put himself in the plate. He offered his whole, living self to God.

Here comes the offering plate. It is in your hands now. What will you do?

We are living sacrifices when we use our bodies, minds, hearts, and strength to serve God and others all day every day. You can spot a person who is a living sacrifice to God by the way he or she pours out self, bringing God's peace, joy, love, healing, and blessing wherever he or she goes.

One word of caution about a living sacrifice: it can very easily wiggle off the altar! You can *say* you give yourself sacrificially to God, and then try to fool yourself and others into believing that you really are all that, though in reality you are living for yourself.

In your daily life, what are you doing for God that is really costing you something? Where in your life is your sacrificial service to God?

We are to give ourselves to him as *holy* sacrifices. When we think of holy things, our minds go to monasteries, celibacy, stained glass, and lists of rules to follow. Where I grew up, the boys would say, "I don't smoke. Don't cuss. Don't chew. Don't go with girls who do." Holiness is not legalistic attempts at piety. Biblical holiness is not squeaky-clean perfection.

The word *holy* means set apart for God's use. My wife Cheryl has beautiful celadon dishes from Thailand. They are set apart for use when special people come to supper. Come on over, and we'll pull out the celadon and treat you as a special guest.

If you are a follower of Christ, you are set apart for God's special use. God sees the heart, and yearns to find people who have set themselves aside as belonging to him. Those are the ones who truly worship him. Are you a useful, clean vessel for his service?

We are to give ourselves as *acceptable* sacrifices. True worshippers always want to know, "God, is my life pleasing to you in this moment? Is what I am doing now, what I am thinking now, acceptable to you?" We do not set the standard of acceptability. God does. He is looking at human hearts to find a person who fully delights in pleasing him.

David, even after having committed adultery and murder, was a man after God's own heart because he genuinely repented and wanted his life to belong completely to God. That is the person who is truly worshipping. Is that person you?

> *Worship is a lifestyle of spirit-responsiveness to God's truth.*

Are you stuck? Rethink your body. Rethink worship.

RETHINK FITTING IN SOCIALLY

> Don't copy the behavior
> and customs of this world.
> (Rom 12:2 NLT)

We all want to belong. We want to fit in. Even the most introverted person desires relational connectivity. However, we are prone to compromise our beliefs for the sake of social acceptance.

Don't become so adapted to your culture that you fit in with everybody without even thinking. The culture will drag you down to the lowest level of immaturity and immorality. Following God will lift you up, bring his best to you, and create selfless maturity in you. In what ways are you tempted to conform to the ways of the world around you?

Stinkin' society thinkin': "Everybody is doing it."

Self-talk: "Just because other people stoop that low, that doesn't mean I will. I'm saving myself for marriage, and giving my pure self to my spouse as a beautiful gift. And I'm holding out to find someone who is doing the same for me."

Stinkin' society thinkin': "If your spouse is not meeting your needs, find someone on the side who will."

Self-talk: "If our marriage is not sizzling, then I have homework. How can I meet my spouse's needs? When can the two of us get away for a just-the-two-of-us vacation?"

> *Don't let the world pressure you into thinking like the world.*

Stinkin' society thinkin': "This church is not meeting our needs. Let's find others in the church who agree, and together we'll either rebel against church leadership or go find another church that has our kind of music, our kind of preaching, and our kind of people."

Self-talk: "The Lord is the one who meets my spiritual needs. He can speak to me through whatever kind of music, preaching, and people that he chooses. I worship him. I hope that my worship of him is pleasing to him. Worship is not about pleasing me."

At the core of human culture is the advancement of self. Follow the culture, and here is what's on your mind:

"What's in it for me?" *Stinkin' society thinkin'*.

"If I'm going to get anywhere in this world, I have to scramble to get ahead of others." *Stinkin' society thinkin'*.

"Gotta hang on to all I've got even if it hurts someone along the way." *Stinkin' society thinkin'*.

"Oh, but if I don't do what my friends expect, they won't be my friends anymore." *Stinkin' society thinkin'*.

Don't let the world around you pressure you into thinking like the world thinks.

What you feel and see will determine your mind-set *unless* your mind is set on truth, which will determine *how* you see and feel.

Stuck? Rethink for a change! Rethink your body. Rethink worship. Rethink fitting in socially.

RETHINK THINKING

> Let God transform you into a new person
> by changing the way you think.
> (Rom 12:2)

"I am powerless to change." *Stinkin' thinkin'*.

"I am who I am. That's that." *Stinkin' thinkin'*.

"My future will be just like my past. I am stuck." *Stinkin' thinkin'*.

There is a fountain of life-changing water flowing down from heaven, but your bucket may not be under its flow. Your bucket may be stuck in the corner of stubborn, self-reliance. That's such a barren corner. Move the bucket of your mind and place it under the powerful flow of God's truth and life-changing power.

What will happen? A metamorphosis of your mind! A radical change in the way you think!

With your bucket in the dry, self-reliant corner, you think of work as a way to earn money, provide for your family, and develop skills. When there is no raise, no new skill to learn, no advancement, you are stuck.

However, with your bucket under the joy-splashing truth of God's living water, you know that God has positioned you right where you are at work because the guy at the next desk is seeking the truth, and is asking you about what you believe. You go to work every day eager to relate to others in a way that shows how real God is to you. You know that you are on the job to live out God's power and grace among people who desperately need him. Instead of working for self-advancement, you work for his will to be done through you.

God wants to pour his undeserved favor all over your life, but you have to cooperate with him by getting the bucket of your brain under his flow of grace. Let him rain grace on you!

Stuck? Rethink for a change! Rethink your body. Rethink worship. Rethink fitting in socially. Rethink thinking.

RETHINK LIFE

> Then you will learn to know God's will for you,
> which is good and pleasing and perfect.
> (Rom 12:2)

There is no life as empty as the self-centered life. Are you bound and determined to live life your way? Deep down, though you believe God exists, does it seem he is unconcerned about the details of your daily life? Though you still go through churchy motions, have you secretly given up on God and chosen to take your life into your own hands? Has God disappointed you? What would it take for you to be willing to pray this prayer?

> Lord, I am willing
> To receive what you give;
> To lack what you withhold;
> To relinquish what you take;
> To suffer what you inflict;
> To be what you require.

Stop trying to make the universe and those in it follow your orders. Surrender of expectations brings you to the place where you truly rethink life and simply desire nothing more than following whatever his plan for you might be. God really does have an awesome, personalized plan for you. In fact, he had the plan for your life mapped out before you were even born!

You can learn to know his very specific, personalized will for your daily life! Finding and following his plan begins with stripping off that old motionless wallpaper that surrounds your mind. You've been staring at "stuck" for too long. Put in its place new God-given visions and dreams that move with high-density life action.

You will find that he renovates the walls of your mind. He reconstructs your life. You will enter into a lifestyle where you personally experience the presence, power, and leadership of God in your life.

Life will become a sacred trust granted to you daily. God will make clear his personal will for your life, and it will be . . .

. . . *good!* "Now this is what I was born to do!"

. . . *pleasing!* "I like this! I can tell God likes me doing it!"

. . . *perfect!* "I am now reaching my life's destiny."

Stuck? Rethink for a change!

STUCK? RETHINK FOR A CHANGE!

Questions for Reflection and Discussion

Read Romans 12:1–2 in several versions.
After reflecting on the chapter you read, which of the following rethinks do you need the most? Why?
___ Rethink my body
___ Rethink worship
___ Rethink fitting in socially
___ Rethink thinking
___ Rethink life

In what ways are you honoring God with your body?

In what ways are you dishonoring him with your body?

Finish this definition: Worship is . . .

Worship is not worship unless there is sacrifice. In what ways are you giving sacrificially to God?

Describe a time when you gave in to peer pressure. If you had it to do over again, what would you do differently?

Our minds can be compared to a bucket, either sitting in a dry corner of self-reliance or positioned to catch the flow of God's life-changing water. Where is your bucket?

Life is a sacred trust, granted to you daily by God. What on earth are you doing for heaven's sake?

Write out your own prayer to God:

> *If we are to conquer strongholds, we must first be conquered by Christ.*

> *Anyone who sets himself up as "religious" by talking a good game is self-deceived. This kind of religion is hot air and only hot air.*
>
> *James 1:26*
> *The Message*

7

Preparing to Take Down a Stronghold

JERICHO WAS A STRONGHOLD, a fortress with strong defenses, complete with secure sources of supplies, and organized with well-prepared operation procedures. Surrounding the fort was a wall forty feet high and fourteen feet wide. The stronghold was as sturdy as could be.

What happened at Jericho, and the *way* it happened is utterly amazing. Despite the seeming absurdity of God's preparation instructions, the people followed his word exactly, and the bricks of Jericho's walls became like jello! The walls came a tumblin' *down*!

> *Fit every thought into the structure of a life shaped by Christ.*

The archaeological evidence dated back to the time of the event recorded in the Old Testament book of Joshua affirms the destruction of the stronghold of Jericho as an actual historical event.[1] Not only is it literally true, the taking down of that stronghold also provides us with God's way of dealing with strongholds today.

God's way is *not* the way we might choose. The weapons with which we fight mental strongholds are not the weapons of this world. We don't fight a physical fight. The battle for our minds is spiritual warfare. The

---

1. New York Times, Feb. 22, 1990: Battle of Jericho, by John Noble Wilford. Even without archaeological evidence, the events of the Bible should be taken as literally true unless the Bible itself describes them as figurative.

enemy is powerful. However, to demolish strongholds, we have God's far greater power.

We use powerful God-tools to smash warped philosophies, demolish deceptive arguments based on human reason, take hostage seemingly lofty thoughts that set themselves up against our experiencing God, and reign in every single loose thought. As Christ followers, we fit every thought, emotion, and impulse into the structure of life shaped by Christ (2 Cor 10:3–5).

A mental stronghold is a thought pattern that keeps us from living by God's truth. The result of a stronghold is spiritual bondage in our lives. The deceiver repeats thoughts to us over and over, until those thoughts become our own, and we start repeating them to ourselves.

"I messed up, and now my life is ruined." *Stinkin' thinkin'*.

"This problem is just way too big and too complex. There is no way forward." *Stinkin' thinkin'*.

"Why won't people listen to me? They should know I have all the answers." *Stinkin' prideful thinkin'*.

"Other people play with fire and get burned. I'm different. I can play with fire and not get burned." *Stinkin' thinkin'*.

These and many other strongholds such as fear, anger, lust, anxiety, selfishness, insecurity, and shame grow deep roots into our psyches. Tearing down such strongholds is no easy task. Before beginning, there is much preparation to be done.

As the people of God prepared to take down the stronghold of Jericho, God had them go through some very unusual preparation exercises. An onlooker might have thought, "How bizarre!"

Is there a stronghold gripping your mind? Are you willing to do whatever preparation God says is necessary for breaking down the stronghold? Will you prepare as he says, even if it seems strange to you and to others?

What is involved in God's way of preparing you to demolish the strongholds in your life? Here are six steps in preparing to take down strongholds.

LET THE GREATNESS OF GOD SILENCE THE ENEMY

Joshua and the people of God were on their way to the land God had promised to them. Along the way, they had encountered and overcome many obstacles, including hunger, thirst, their own rebellion, complaining, and enemy attacks.

Preparing to Take Down a Stronghold

Today many of us have been delivered out of the slavery of sin, and yet we have not quite arrived at that land of blessedness, where we live out the promises God has offered to us. The problem lies in the way we think.

In Joshua 5, the people finally arrived *near* the promised land, and approached the Jordan River, which was overflowing its banks. God directed Joshua to have the priests carrying the ark of the covenant, the symbol of God's presence, to walk straight into the water. As the feet of the priests touched the water's edge, the water above that point backed up a great distance away. The riverbed dried up, and the people crossed on dry ground! The people of God were now on the west side of the Jordan River in the promised land.

> When all the Amorite kings west of the Jordan
> and all the Canaanite kings
> who lived along the Mediterranean coast
> heard how the Lord had dried up the Jordan River
> so the people could cross,
> they lost heart and were paralyzed with fear.
> (Josh 5:1 NLT)

The enemies heard of God's great power, and their knees started knocking. They thought they were protected by that great surging river. However, God did what common sense said was impossible. He removed the seemingly impossible barrier, so the stronghold could be taken down. God can make the biggest barriers seem puny. He still parts the waters.

If you are a follower of Christ, you have an enemy. The enemy may cause barriers in front of you to seem bigger than life. He is the one seeking to distort your thinking and destroy God's path for your life. In fact, if you got up this morning and didn't meet the devil face to face, it might be a sign the two of you are heading in the same direction!

The enemy is powerful, but there are ways to immobilize him. He cannot stand to hear of God's greatness and power. Praising the Lord Jesus makes Satan shiver with fear. When the enemy puts an intimidating river between you and God's promises, ask God to part the waters. Watch God do the impossible!

When he does, you must speak out about the great power of God. Watch the enemy's knees knock. Satan's little demonizers will tremble in terror as you praise God for his greatness. When you start to focus on God's greatness, the spiritual oppression and deception wrapped around your mind start to loosen their grip on your thinking.

Like a loud, raging river, Satan's voice tries to block you from God's promises. What is the enemy repeatedly saying to you? Today, let the greatness of God silence the enemy.

You're not worthy of grace! Silence!

Getting out of your wilderness is impossible. Give up! Silence!

Just try to cross that wild river. You'll drown! Are you crazy? Silence!

There's no future for you. Just crawl in a hole. Silence! Today, let the greatness of God silence the enemy.

Do you recognize the ways in which God may have already parted the waters for you? Are you praising him for his great power at work in your life? Have you marked down in your mind the dry river crossings of your life, giving God the glory?

Pray God's word back to him. *God, in Isaiah 43:2, you promise that when I go through deep waters, you will be with me. When I walk through the fires of oppression, I will not be burned up. The flames will not consume me. You are an awesome God!*

Quit focusing on your problems, and start praising God! Stop depending on your puny strength and start relying fully on God's miraculous power. Watch the enemy cower in nervous sweat.

The first step in preparing to take down a stronghold is to let the greatness of God silence the enemy. The second step is most unusual.

LET GOD CIRCUMCISE YOUR HEART

Strategically, you would think the best plan of attack would be to advance on enemy territory immediately after the unexpected crossing of the Jordan River. The enemy was staring at a mob of a million or more people. At the front of the mob of Jews were forty thousand soldiers, ready to attack.

It was a perfect time for rapid advance. However, that is not at all what God had his people do in preparing to take down a stronghold. What did he have them do at that pivotal time?

> At that time the Lord told Joshua,
> "Make flint knives and circumcise
> this second generation of Israelites" . . .
> The Israelites had traveled in the wilderness

> for forty years until all the men who were old enough
> to fight in battle when they left Egypt had died . . .
> So Joshua circumcised their sons . . .
> After all the males had been circumcised,
> they rested in the camp until they were healed.
> (Josh 5:2–8)

The enemy never would have expected them to be able to cross the Jordan at flood stage. It would have been a perfect time to attack immediately. However, God delayed and even crippled his own people, by having the men circumcised.

Circumcision is minor surgery on males to remove their foreskin. For Jews, it is a symbol of identifying with God and his people, a purifying ritual of dedication to God. Circumcision should have been done when the male child was eight days old, but here it is performed on grown men.

Why now? Why go into battle so vulnerable and still in pain? God disabled them from action at the very moment they were ready to spring into action. God reminded them victory is not by their own might, but by the Lord's Spirit.

Pray God's word back to him. *Lord, you say in 2 Corinthians 12:9 that your grace is enough for me. Your power works best in my weakness. So I will stay weak and let the power of Christ be strong in me.*

If you are to bring down strongholds, spiritual preparation is more important than any human advantage. If you are to be properly prepared for spiritual warfare against mental strongholds, you must rest in your own weakness, let God circumcise your heart, and let *him* give you marching orders for battle. The battle belongs to the Lord. Strongholds are spiritual, and are only overcome by God's power.

> When you came to Christ, you were circumcised,
> but not by a physical procedure.
> It was a spiritual procedure—
> the cutting away of your sinful nature.
> (Col 2:11 NLT)

Coming to Christ means coming to his cross, asking forgiveness of your sin. However, the cross is not just about forgiveness. It's about breaking the chains of sin and empowering you for purity.

Whoopin' Up on Stinkin' Thinkin'

The circumcising knife of Christ is ready to perform brain surgery. Identify the precise unwanted growth in your mind. What is the stronghold? Is it pride, worry, envy, or lust? Whatever it is, let his knife cut away every unhelpful, deceptive thought in your mind. Let him surgically remove every area of your heart that inhibits spiritual growth.

> *The cross empowers you for purity.*

Do you boldly march into battles in your own strength? Are you looking for self-worth outside of Christ? Do you find your identity to be more in your position or possessions than in Christ? Do you pride yourself in being a self-made person? Have him cut out that false base of worth.

Circumcision is an identity marker, showing the person belongs to God. Victory over strongholds comes when you have a clear identity of whose you are.

Though Christ removed the shackles of sin at your salvation, the human heart is still prone to wander away from God. Are you in a compromising relationship? Give him permission to perform heart surgery and cut it out.

What has a hold over your mind? Greed? Power hunger? Shame? Anger? Fear? Hopelessness? Whatever it is, take that stronghold before Christ's knife for circumcision.

In 1831, Jamaican slaves were finally set free. Someone brought caskets to the event. The slaves ceremoniously put their shackles in the caskets and buried them. However, some slaves could not wrap their minds around being free, and remained in servitude as if they were still under the bondage of slavery.

Have you placed your faith in Christ as Lord of your life? Jesus Christ has set you free! He has removed the shackles. You are a new, free creation in Christ Jesus! God has broken the power of the "flesh" that was in charge of you. Now his Spirit within you seeks to be in charge, as you allow him. Don't go back to the fleshly shackles. You are free. You are empowered for pure living for your new Master!

Circumcision cuts away the unnecessary. What in your heart and mind needs circumcised?

How do you prepare for taking down a stronghold? Let the greatness of God silence the enemy. Let God circumcise your heart.

Preparing to Take Down a Stronghold

LET GOD ROLL AWAY YOUR SHAME

> Then the Lord said to Joshua,
> "Today I have rolled away the shame
> of your slavery in Egypt." So that place
> has been called Gilgal[2] to this day.
> (Josh 5:9)

The people of God had lived shameful lives as slaves in Egypt. Even after being freed from slavery, they became homeless drifters in the wilderness, without a sense of identity.

Satan would keep us ever thinking that we should be ashamed. He says it as clearly as Gomer Pyle, "Shame! Shame! Shame!"

> *On the cross, Jesus was shamed so we don't have to be.*

Yes, we are guilty of sin before God and man. We deserve blame and shame. However, on the cross Jesus not only took the punishment for our sin, he took on our shame as well. Out of pure love for us, God himself endured a shameful death.

The cross was a torturous death reserved only for the most notable criminals. Crucifixion was naked, convulsing, fly-infested slow death with grim humiliation. God the Father himself turned his back on God the Son during that moment of God-forsaken injustice. He bore our shame so we don't have to!

If that is true, why do some followers of Christ still keep potentially shameful things a secret? We believe we are keeping a secret, when in fact the secret is keeping us. We fear condemnation. However, neither the fear of condemnation nor the condemnation itself is from God. *There is now no condemnation for those who are in Christ Jesus* (Rom 8:1). For those set free in Christ, blame, shame, and condemnation are potential mental strongholds. They seek to recapture what was once Satan's mental hold over us. Strongholds seek to enslave us.

One of the most major causes of strongholds is the mental recycling of shameful memories. Shame is a favorite tool in the devil's workshop. What are you feeling shameful about? Take it to the cross, and hear God say, "Today, I have rolled away your shame." Say it! "Today, God has rolled away my shame." Say it again, louder. "Today, You have rolled away my shame, God."

---

2. "Gilgal" sounds like the Hebrew word, "gal," which means to roll away.

Repentance, a turning from self to Christ-centered living, introduces us to grace, the undeserved favor of God. Repentance is a genuine sorrow over sin designed by God to convict us and lead us back to him. When anything else makes us have sorrow over sin, it feels like the warden has come to lock us back up. When grace gets involved in our sin, the truth of repentance reveals a fabulous world of brokenness turned into beauty without shame.

It's time to prepare for taking down strongholds. Let the greatness of God silence the enemy. Let God circumcise your heart. Let God roll away the shame in your life.

CELEBRATE THE LAMB

> While the Israelites were camped at Gilgal
> on the plains of Jericho,
> they celebrated the Passover
> on the evening of the fourteenth day of the first month—
> the month that marked their exodus from Egypt.
> (Josh 5:10)

The first Passover came about when God was pressing Pharaoh to let his people go free. God sent ten plagues, with the final plague being the death of every firstborn son in Egypt. However, God's people were told that if they would take the blood of a lamb, and put it over the door of the house, the death angel would "pass over" their house without incident.

From the Egyptian marble mansions early that morning came gut-wrenching cries of the mothers. Oh, the grief of losing a first son!

In a Jewish slave shack, a firstborn son may have said, "Daddy, the death angel is coming tonight for all firstborn. That's me. Am I going to die tonight?"

"No son, the blood of the lamb has us covered."

Though the Jews were to celebrate the Passover annually, there is no record of their having done so for thirty-nine years of wandering in the wilderness. Now on entering the promised land, it was the first time for most of them to observe the Passover. What a powerful object lesson in being saved from death through the blood of the Lamb.

Jesus is the Lamb of God who takes away the sin of all those in the world who trust him! Look! The death angel is coming straight for you.

Preparing to Take Down a Stronghold

There is no way to escape. Suddenly, Jesus steps in front of you, and says, "Step aside. I'll die for you." Celebrate the blood of the Lamb! A tremendous price has been paid for you, and God says you are worth it.

Picture a big red price tag draped around your neck, as if you were for sale. What kind of price would you put on yourself? How much are you worth? The price tag on you is red because of the blood of Jesus shed for you. The price tag cannot be made lengthy enough to include all the digits needed to show what price God has placed on you. You are of infinite value to him. Celebrate the blood of the Lamb.

So much of our stinkin' thinkin' simply needs to be covered by the blood of the Lamb. Let your guilt and shame be covered by his blood. Jesus took your guilt and shame on himself on the cross. Put your fear and anxiety under the blood. In placing your trust in Christ, you became a child of God. He loves you enough to die for you. He will take care of you. Take your Satan-inflicted inferiority complex and wash it under the blood. Say it aloud: "I am of infinite value to God."

> *Take your Satan-inflicted inferiority complex and wash it under the blood.*

In preparing to take down strongholds, let the greatness of God silence the enemy. Let God circumcise your heart. Roll away the shame in your life. Celebrate the blood of the Lamb.

TRUST GOD TO PROVIDE DURING CHANGE

Change, even needed change, can bring out the worst in us. This is especially true when bringing down strongholds. "If I no longer have self-pity as the theme of my life, what will I have to say when I'm around other people? What would I do without my habit of reminding everyone how pitiful I am?"

When a person who has always been blind receives sight, the change is overwhelming. There is so much brightness. Dark, shadowy areas are a new concept. Depth perception is an entirely new reality. Before, everything was recognized by feel, but now everything must be recognized by sight without feel.

Very few of us readily embrace change. It seems the only person who genuinely likes change is a baby in a dirty diaper!

Our negative reaction to change tells us we have been operating under the illusion that we are in charge of our life's direction, that we deceive ourselves into thinking we are the captain of our own ships.

For forty years, God's people had been provided daily room service by God. For breakfast, they had manna bagels. For lunch, it was manna burgers. Supper brought manna soufflé. Then after crossing the Jordan, all of a sudden there was huge change. No more manna.

> The very next day
> they began to eat unleavened bread
> and roasted grain harvested from the land.
> No manna appeared that day,
> and it was never seen again.
> So from that time on the Israelites
> ate from the crops of Canaan.
> (Josh 5:11–12)

"What? No more manna? We've always done things the manna way. If we don't have our manna back, we will starve! What are you trying to do to us, inflicting this change on us? We *must* get things back to the way they were."

Change is a fact of life. Previously hidden strongholds often become evident during change; strongholds like trust in tradition instead of trust in God.

God says, "You trusted me to give you manna. Now trust me to provide for you through the land." The source of their strength changed from manna to grain. When tearing down a stronghold, be prepared for the source of your inner strength to change.

The pillar of cloud by day and the fire by night ceased when they entered the promised land. God was challenging them to change from living by sight to living by faith.

Without us even being aware of it, a mental stronghold calls us to rely on it for the strength in our lives. Lust says, "I will provide what you need most." Fear says, "There is a mean world out there. Stick with me and I will help you stay clear of fearful things." We start to place false trust in our stronghold.

> *Make a shift from dependence on deceptive strongholds to dependence on stronghold-busting truth.*

Preparing to Take Down a Stronghold

It will seem awkward at first, but you must make a mental shift away from dependence on the stronghold and toward dependence on the Lord and his stronghold-busting truth. You will soon see that the strength God gives is wholesome and health inducing, whereas the flawed, sick strength the stronghold provides keeps you spiritually, and perhaps physically, anemic.

Changes in life are great times to trust God to provide the resources you need, though he will likely do so in a different way than he did previously. The variety provided by the land is actually better than the same manna every day. God brings change into your life to bring good things into your life and remove things out of your life that are no longer helpful. Though that's tough to see in the middle of change, trust him.

God says, "Trust me through this change. Trust me through the next change as well." God walks faithfully with us through every change and each moment of difficulty. God provides the strength for the change that comes when strongholds crumble.

> *God says, "Trust me through this change."*

Craig Barnes of Washington, DC, says,

> When I was a child, my father brought home twelve-year-old Roger, whose parents had died from drug overdose. My parents raised him. It was very difficult for Roger to adjust to an environment free of heroin addiction. I heard my parents say to Roger, "No. That's not how we behave in this family."
>
> "No. Don't scream or fight or hurt others to get your way. We expect you to show respect in this family." In time, Roger began to change. He didn't make the changes in order to join the family. He was part of the family by the grace of my father. He had to work hard to accept change, but the love he received motivated him to do so.[3]

God has adopted you into his family by his grace. The Holy Spirit often says, "Change! That's not how we act in this family." You don't change in order to become part of the family. You change because you are motivated by the Father's love for you.

Before Christ, you were in Egypt as the slave of sin. You were wandering in the wilderness of rebellion. God has taken you out of Egypt and out of the wilderness. Now you must take Egypt and the wilderness out of your

---

3. Nationalpres.org/sermons

mind and out of your hearts. Now you are in the promised land of God's blessings. Stop longing for manna. Instead, enjoy the land of promise.

How do you prepare for taking down a stronghold? Let the greatness of God silence the enemy. Let God circumcise your heart. Let God roll away your shame. Celebrate the blood of the Lamb. Trust God to provide during change.

BE CONQUERED BY THE LORD

Joshua went ahead of the people and took a look at Jericho. As he viewed the towering fortress, it is not difficult to imagine Joshua's thoughts.

Hmm . . . How high is that wall? How many ladders do we need to climb over it? How many hinges are on those big front gates? How many battering rams do we need to bust through those gates?

While sizing up Jericho, all of a sudden, Joshua found himself falling face down to the ground.

> When Joshua was near the town of Jericho,
> he looked and saw a man standing in front of him
> with sword in hand. Joshua went up to him
> and demanded, "Are you friend or foe?"
> "Neither one," he replied.
> "I am the commander of the Lord's army."
> (Josh 5:13–14)

How strange! All of a sudden, standing before Joshua was an unrecognizable armed creature. Fearless, Joshua boldly approached the man. "Are you fighting for me, or against me?"

"Neither. I'm in charge. Joshua, this is not your battle. The battle belongs to me. I'm the commander in charge. You are relieved of your duty."

Joshua fell on his face and worshipped.

I am just like Joshua. In my own human strength, I size up my life's challenges. I assume the battle is mine and I must fight bravely. I must determine who is on my side and who isn't. I hope that God will be on *my* side as well. I might even pray and ask him, "God, are you on my side? Are you *even* fighting for me?"

It's then that I hear him reply, "My child, you are asking the wrong question. It's time for you to do some whoopin' up on your stinkin' thinkin'. You think the battle belongs to you. However, the battle belongs to me! The

Preparing to Take Down a Stronghold

question is not, 'Is God on your side?' The question is, 'Are you on God's side?'"

Notice the four ways that Joshua responded to the commander.

> At this, Joshua fell with his face to the ground
> in reverence. "I am at your command,"
> Joshua said. "What do you want your servant to do?"
> The commander of the Lord's army replied,[4]
> "Take off your sandals,
> for the place where you are standing is holy."
> And Joshua did as he was told.
> (Josh 5:14–15)

First, Joshua fell face down to the ground. Such a posture was taken when a general was surrendering to the victorious general. The posture of surrender was not merely a bowing of the knees to the ground and tilting the head forward. The one surrendering would continue further down until the entire body was lying flat, face down before the conquering commander.

Have you come to the point of realizing your life's battles are not yours? Do you have a vision in your mind of the commander of your battles? Have you fallen completely flat, face down in surrender to the commander in charge?

Like Joshua, if you want to conquer the strongholds in your life, you must worship before warring, bow before battling, and submit before serving. Do it now, without hesitation. If you will, I encourage you to actually fall flat, face down before the Lord right now and fully surrender yourself to him. The rest of this book can wait until you do just that.

> *Secular battles are won only by realizing the sacred presence of Christ.*

Really, don't read any farther until you have done so. Everything else will wait.

Second, Joshua made a clear commitment of himself to the Lord's commands. "I am at your command." Do you consider his commands to be merely optional guidance? Do you live by your own thoughts, plans and

---

4. The phrase "Commander of the Lord's Army" is used 250 times in the Old Testament. The "army of the Lord" describes an invincible army of heaven's host of angels ready to do spiritual warfare on our behalf and bring down strongholds. The fact that the Commander did not correct Joshua when he fell down in worship likely means this was an actual theophany: an appearance of God.

impulses, or by first seeking what the commander commands of you? Have you searched a red-letter Bible to read the words of Christ and circle his commands? Have you compared your life to his commands?

Third, Joshua requested specific directions before moving. "What do you want me to do?" How long has it been since you have asked the Lord that question? If you were to ask for the Lord's specific guidance before acting all throughout each day, how might your life be different?

Fourth, Joshua became aware that secular battles are won only by realizing the sacred presence of God. The commander taught Joshua this reality by simply having Joshua take off his shoes. For God's child, life's secular battlefields must be seen as holy ground.

I love the vision of the new church plant in New Braunfels, Texas, called "Epic Life." They meet at an indoor batting cage park on Sunday morning, and in homes and businesses during the week. Here is their vision: to see Christ followers transforming everyday places into sacred spaces where people can connect to Christ.[5] The secular world is sacred ground. Take off your shoes.

If we are to conquer strongholds, we must first be conquered by Christ. God wants to reveal himself personally to you and take command of your battle against strongholds.

> We become the plan we follow.

Is God revealing to you your self-directed tendency? How do you respond? How about responding like this?

Today, the greatness of God silences the enemy.
Today, I let God circumcise my heart.
Today, God rolls away my shame.
Today, I celebrate the blood of the Lamb.
Today, I trust God to provide during change.
Today, I am conquered by Christ.

---

5. Facebook: Epic Life NB

PREPARING TO TAKE DOWN STRONGHOLDS

Reflection and Discussion

Prayerfully review Joshua chapter 5. Fill in the blanks and make comments in the spaces provided.

Read Joshua 5:1
"The enemy speaks to me, saying _____, but today, the greatness of God silences the enemy."

Read Joshua 5:2–8
"My heart has been filled with _____, but today, I let God circumcise my heart."

Read Joshua 5:9
"I have felt ashamed about _____, but today, God has rolled away my shame."

Read Joshua 5:10
"I have been a slave to _____, but today, I celebrate the cleansing blood of the Lamb.

Read Joshua 5:11–12
"I have been worried about _____, but today, I trust God to provide during change."

Read Joshua 5:13–15.
"I have pretended to be in charge of _____, but today, I am conquered by Christ."

*Stop deceiving yourselves.
If you think you are wise
by this world's standards,
you need to become a fool
to be truly wise.
For the wisdom of this world
is foolishness to God.
As the Scriptures say,
"He traps the wise in the snare
of their own cleverness."
And again,
"The Lord knows the
thoughts of the wise;
he knows they are worthless."*

*1 Corinthians 3:18–20 NLT
Quoting Job 5:13; Psalm 94:11*

8

Principles for Overcoming Strongholds

GOD'S PEOPLE HAD FINALLY come out of the wilderness and were preparing to possess the promised land. However, there stood before them the fortress Jericho. If that stronghold could be conquered, the good land of Canaan was theirs to enjoy!

Perhaps you have come out of the wilderness of sin through faith in Christ. God has a great place of promise for you. However, there may stand between you and his promises a stronghold. It is a spiritual stronghold; a thought pattern of deception that takes root in your personality and determines your values and behavior. Faith in Christ is the first step in an ongoing process of your mind being transformed by God's Spirit within you.

Many strongholds go unrecognized. Other strongholds, though recognized, are strangely valued as "needed" in life. Whatever deceptions linger loosely in your mind, they are strongholds which stand between you and your ability to enjoy the victorious life of God's promises. They must be taken captive and demolished (2 Cor 10:3–5).

What is your Jericho? Are you ready for the walls of your Jericho to come a tumblin' down? Here are eight biblically based principles to help you overcome strongholds.

PRINCIPLE ONE:
BELIEVE THE VICTORY IS ALREADY WON!

> Now the gates of Jericho were tightly shut
> because the people were afraid of the Israelites.
> No one was allowed to go out or in.
> But the LORD said to Joshua,
> "I have given you Jericho,
> its king, and all its strong warriors."
> (Josh 6:1–2 NLT)

What is your Jericho? What stronghold do you face? Are things like shame, anger, lust, inferiority, pride, addiction, or depression a part of your life? Though it may seem to you like that stronghold is insurmountably strong, and though the reality of Jericho's presence may put fear in you, it's time to face up to the facts. You have no reason to fear your Jericho. Your Jericho has great reason to fear you!

The mental stronghold that has set itself up so high somehow knows that the Lord God Almighty is fighting for you. The stronghold you fear actually fears that its time with you is just about over. Though your Jericho is shutting the gates tight as your great God approaches, your stronghold is already on its way down.

You are not fighting *for* victory. You are fighting *as a victor*! You are *not* a victim. You are more than a conqueror through *Christ* (Rom 8:37). Jesus is the victor. He has *already* won the battle over Satan on the cross. Satan knows he is already defeated. He is daily aware of what defeat feels like. He's just trying to fool us into thinking that *we* are defeated.

> *Jesus has already won the battle over Satan on the cross.*

You and I must develop a habit crucial to bringing down strongholds. We must recognize our stinkin' thinkin', and call it out. We must then search God's Word for truth that corrects that stinkin' thinkin', and pray God's word back to him.

Here's an example of a stronghold:

"There's just too much in this world that seems to be working against me." *Stinkin' thinkin'!*

You can correct such a thought by praying God's word back to him. *God, even though life is tough, your word says in Romans 8:31 that since you are for me, who can be against me? Lord, I know that the enemy is messing with my mind, and forming his attack on my inner man. However, I claim your promise from Isaiah 54:17 that no weapon formed against me will stand.*

Don't think for a minute that the mental stronghold you face cannot be overcome. Instead, believe that through the cross of Christ, God has already given the victory (1 Cor 15:57; 2 Cor 5:17–18; Rom 6:14; 8:11; 8:37; Heb 7:25–27; Col 2:15; Gal 2:20; 1 Pet 3:18–22; Rev 12:11)!

PRINCIPLE TWO: ACCEPT A NEW PLAN WITHOUT RESISTANCE

> "You and your fighting men should march
> around the town once a day for six days.
> Seven priests will walk ahead of the Ark,
> each carrying a ram's horn. On the seventh day
> you are to march around the town seven times,
> with the priests blowing the horns.
> When you hear the priests give one long blast
> on the rams' horns, have all the people shout
> as loud as they can.
> Then the walls of the town will collapse,
> and the people can charge straight into the town."
> So Joshua called together the priests and said,
> "Take up the Ark of the LORD's Covenant,
> and assign seven priests to walk in front of it,
> each carrying a ram's horn."
> (Josh 6:3–6 NLT)

What a strange plan for bringing down the towering walls of Jericho. God sending his people into battle with only a strange wood box called the ark of the covenant and seven ram horn trumpets is like sending a Navy seal team in with a Superman lunch box and water pistols. The plan made absolutely no common sense.

Imagine being Joshua. You hear God tell you his most unusual plan. You think, "How in the world are the people going to react to this plan?" Already, the men are hurting physically from circumcision. They are eager to heal quickly, put on their shields, grab their swords, and charge. Now

God says to tell them they don't get to initiate the conquest by physical attack.

Joshua told them the plan. Amazingly, they followed. They may not have even known the plan fully. They just followed their marching orders, day after day. They could have said, "We've never done it that way before. That's not in our constitution. Therefore, we must take a vote on this."

> *We become the plans we follow. From what source do your plans originate?*

George Barna says that churches tend to rely on their past, and then become unwilling to make the changes that today's challenges require.[1] It is dangerous for a church to resist a new God-given plan. Resisting God's plan is what keeps churches from entering into God's land of promise. Resistance to following a new plan leads churches into decline. In a short time, a church can descend from boldly claiming enemy territory while marching forward, to settling for the comfort of becoming a fried chicken fellowship club.

> *Are you willing to let go of your plan and follow his?*

We are resistant to change in part because we have confused methods with the message. We tend to think the method we grew up with is sacred. However, methods change (1 Cor 9:21–23). Only the message of salvation in Christ is sacred. Victory comes when we accept a new method God reveals.

We become the plan we follow. From what source do your plans originate? Do you make your own plans? Does your plan ensure that things will never change? Have you stopped to consider that God is on the move, and if you are to be in step with him, you must stop following your own stuck-in-the-mud plans and accept his plan without resistance?

His plan, though it may seem strange to you, is to use his own power to conquer the enemy and bless you with his fulfilled promises. Refusing his plan keeps you wandering in the wilderness of self-directed living. Time to choose: resist his plan and live miserably self-directed lives, or start marching to his day-by-day orders, even though you don't know what may happen tomorrow.

---

1. George Barna's book "Turn-Around Churches" is well worth reading.

Principles for Overcoming Strongholds

Do your priorities and goals come from you? Would you be willing to lay down your plans and boldly ask God what his plan is for your life? Would you be willing to follow whatever his plan might be, without resistance?

Churches have strongholds as well. That's when *stinkin' group thinkin'* rebels against God's plan for Christ's church.

Stinkin' entitlement thinkin': "We paid for this here building. And we are gonna choose the style of music, the kind of programs, and the kind of preacher we want. This is *our* church. We decide everything!" If the people of such thinking are actually disciples of Christ, they will sense the Spirit convicting them of such sin. They may respond by grieving the Spirit and continuing in rebellion, or they may search the Scriptures, repent, and pray for forgiveness.

When *stinkin' group thinkin'* infests God's people, it's time to pray God's word back to him: "Lord, forgive our sense of entitlement. Lord Jesus, you tell us in Matthew 16:18 that the church belongs to *you*. We have acted like owners instead of stewards. Forgive us. You tell us in Colossians 1:18 that you, Christ, are the head of your body, the church. As members of your body, we have encouraged body parts to act independently of you, the head. Please cut out such cancer from your body. You alone are entitled to have your way among us."

Whether on the group level or the individual level, *whoopin' up on stinkin' thinkin'* requires you to stop following your old plan. Accept God's new plan without resistance. In others words, you must not only be *willing* to change, you must actually *accept* change. You must not only accept change. You must *embrace* change as God's superior plan for taking down the stronghold that now stands before you.

His new plan may involve you in things you would not have chosen for yourself. It may involve sweat and sacrifice. He may put you marching side by side with people you would not have chosen to be with. He may require you to be quiet and think for a change. As he did with Joshua's warriors, he may disable your power in order to pour out his power. Are you willing to let go of your plan and follow his new plan without resistance?

PRINCIPLE THREE:
SILENCE THE VOICE OF UNBELIEF

"Do not shout; do not even talk,"

Whoopin' Up on Stinkin' Thinkin'

Joshua commanded.
"Not a single word from any of you
until I tell you to shout. Then shout!"
(Josh 6:10)

Why did this command need to be given? Because of our inclination to grumble and criticize. Oh, the things they wanted to say to each other as the marched around Jericho day after day! Maybe they whispered their unbelief to each other.

"Can't our leaders see that this plan is going to fail?"

"Silence!"

"Joshua is really making us look foolish!"

"Silence!"

"We were better off back in the wilderness! We don't like this new plan."

"Silence!"

"It's the seventh day now. For goodness' sake, someone please stop this foolish daily march around Jericho."

"Silence!"

"It's hot. And now you say today we must march seven times around? You must be joking!"

"Silence!"

"I deserve better treatment than this. You're going to be hearing from my lawyer."

"Silence!"

If God were to ban all unwholesome speech, how much would we have left to say? He has, you know.

He has banned all unwholesome speech. "Do not let any unwholesome talk come out of your mouths, but only what is helpful for building others up according to their needs, that it may benefit those who listen" (Eph 4:29 NIV).

God knows that we, his people, are prone to rob ourselves of victory by gossiping, nitpicking, criticizing, slandering, and lying. At the root of such stinkiness is pride. The enemy has deceived us into thinking we should set ourselves up as judges of others, and even judges of God's plan for his people.

When you hear unwholesome speech slipping sideways out of the corner of your mouth, hear clearly God's voice saying, "Silence! I have put a permanent ban on words that tear down instead of build up. If you keep talking like that, you won't see Jericho come a tumblin' down!"

Are there voices saying things to you that are *not* based on faith in God? Have you ever considered that instead of repeating to others the unbelief spoken to you, it is possible to silence the voice of unbelief?

Are there marching orders that God has given you, and yet instead of marching obediently, you let the voices of unbelief in your head argue with God about those marching orders?

Would you say instead, "Yes, Lord," and start to march? Even while marching, you may try to reason with God to change the marching orders. How easy is it for you to practice the spiritual discipline of silence?

PRINCIPLE FOUR: KEEP OBEYING EVEN WHEN IT SEEMS FOOLISH

> So the Ark of the LORD was carried
> around the town once that day, and then everyone returned to spend the night in the camp.
> On the second day they again marched
> around the town once and returned to the camp.
> They followed this pattern for six days.
> (Josh 6:11–14 NLT)

Over and over they marched, with exactly the same results each time. What is it called when you do the same thing over and over again, expecting different results? Insanity. They were starting to go crazy, and if it were God's plan they were following then surely *God* himself was crazy![2]

You've been battling with a stronghold for some time now, praying and searching God's word, but still no change. The stronghold prevails. Anger still annoys. Lust still lingers. Discouragement still deceives. Envy still enthralls. Doom still destroys. What should you do?

You have your marching orders already. Keep on getting up every day and putting on your marching boots. However, make sure you are following God's *new* plan for you. Don't revert to your old

> *In faith, before you see the promised victory, shout first.*

---

2. You should read "The Insanity of God," published using the pseudo name Nik Ripken

ways. Get out there and start the daily march around Jericho. True faith is patient. The seventh day is coming. The walls of your stronghold are tumblin' down!

For years, popular music dominated my thoughts. I worked as a rock disc jockey from age fifteen to age twenty-one. Though the work experience helped me mature as a person, the lyrics in the songs did not help my spiritual growth.

Even as a young adult pastor and missionary, I continued to brainlessly memorize the words to popular songs, without evaluating the effect they were having on my thoughts. Finally, after years of allowing such unwholesome influence on my inner man, I began to pray, asking God to take away my love for many of the popular songs focusing on lust, depression over love gone sour, and obsession with someone.

I asked him to help me discern which songs were worth my ears and which were not. Godly friends told me I was becoming unnecessarily legalistic, yet I knew the hold these songs had on my mind.

One day in Georgia, I piled up a tall stack of once-cherished pop music CDs, gave them up to God, and put them out of the house and out of the car. Finally, the stronghold that rock music once held over my mind came tumblin' down. Sometimes strongholds crumble quickly. Sometimes, they are more stubborn. Keep obeying, even when it seems foolish.

Sometimes, it may feel like the stronghold is a mountain in your way. The people of Bihar, India, actually did have a mountain in their way. To get to the market town, the people of Bihar had to walk five miles one way around a mountain.

Bihar villager Ramchandra Das had an idea. With just a chisel and a hammer, he began cutting a tunnel through the mountain in the narrowest part. Many people laughed and told him he was foolish for attempting such a thing. However, when he completed the tunnel, villagers had to walk only one mile round trip. How long did he chisel? Fourteen years!

Fighting a stubborn stronghold? Keep at it, even when it seems foolish. Notice that God's instructions for day seven were different. Day seven was intense. It was time to take radical action to bring the stronghold down. Have you been faithful with the day-by-day march? It may be time to ask God what his day seven radical action is for you to make your Jericho come a tumblin' down.

Principles for Overcoming Strongholds

PRINCIPLE FIVE: SHOUT ABOUT THE VICTORY!

> On the seventh day the Israelites got up at dawn
> and marched around the town as they had done before.
> But this time they went around the town
> seven times.
> The seventh time around,
> as the priests sounded the long blast on their horns,
> Joshua commanded the people,
> "Shout! For the LORD has given you the town!"
> (Josh 6:15–16 NLT)

At what point did Joshua command the people to give the victory shout? Was it after the victory? It was not. Had they seen any change at all in the condition of the walls of Jericho? Any cracks or crumbling? They had not. The city still looked exactly the same as when they had arrived a week prior. What was there to shout about? Seemingly nothing.

Though God had already given them the entire city, *the evidence did not present itself until they started shouting.* Could it be that there are many victories God has already given you, but you refuse to shout, and the result is you have no actualization of the victories?

Here's something worth considering. What if the people of God marching around Jericho had refused to shout as God commanded? Would the walls of Jericho have come a tumblin' down? *Our refusal to be excited over victories God has promised us just might block those victories from actually happening!* Often, God's promises are conditional on our obedience.

What we shout about reveals our true passions and values. What causes you to shout? A football victory? An election result? A Wall Street bell? A weight loss goal met? Since when did it become unspiritual to get excited about what God will do? Unexcited living is faithless living.

Do you and I even know what we should be shouting about? We should shout about the things God says shout about. We should be passionate about what he is passionate about. When you and I wrap our minds around what God puts as his priorities, our mental strongholds begin to come a tumblin' down. God is passionate about people loving him and loving each other. Where is your passion?

Not knowing what to shout about is *not* our only problem with shouting. We don't know *when* to shout. We tend to wait until after we have become convinced of the victory, then shout. Maybe that's why we don't do much shouting. Faith is the substance of things hoped for, not excitement over things having already occurred.

Without faith, it is impossible to please God. God says we should shout first. When we shout before seeing the victory, God is pleased with our faith in him, and he then proceeds to tear down the stronghold before us. Are you waiting for him to tear down your stronghold so you can then shout the victory? Start shouting the victory now, in faith!

PRINCIPLE SIX:
CURSE THE REBUILDING OF THE STRONGHOLD

> "Jericho and everything in it
> must be completely destroyed
> as an offering to the LORD..."
> At that time Joshua invoked this curse:
> "May the curse of the LORD fall on anyone
> who tries to rebuild the town of Jericho.
> At the cost of his firstborn son,
> he will lay its foundation.
> At the cost of his youngest son,
> he will set up its gates."
> (Josh 6:17, 26 NLT)

Trouble came to the camp, just as Joshua warned. Joshua had said that Jericho was never to be rebuilt as a fort. Jericho did become inhabited as a city once again. That in itself was not against what Joshua had prophesied. However, when people attempted to rebuild the fort walls surrounding Jericho, the curse was fulfilled. It happened more than five centuries later, when Ahab was king of Israel.

A man named Hiel of Bethel starting rebuilding the fort walls, and just as Joshua declared, he lost his oldest son when the foundation was being laid, and his youngest son when the gates were being positioned (1 Kgs 16:34).

When God and you have partnered together in the painstaking work of removing a deceptive, crippling mental pattern, don't let that stronghold be rebuilt! Make sure you don't just chop off the top of the weed. Tell God to dig down deep into your heart and mind and pull up every deeply buried root of that stubborn stinkin' thinkin'.

Principles for Overcoming Strongholds

What happens if a person has become convicted over the stronghold of prideful thinking? After months of battling with the deception of being better than others, the stronghold had finally tumbled down. What remains? A big mental vacuum and an empty heart. What is the law of physics concerning a vacuum? A vacuum *will* be filled, by something!

If the person does not intentionally fill the vacuum with God-given things, the enemy rapidly fills the space taken by one stronghold with seven more troublesome strongholds!

In comes *stinkin' inferiority thinkin'*, saying, "You thought you were hot stuff! Now you know the truth: you are nothing but a worm!"

Stinkin' self-absorption thinkin' comes along and says, "Now that you are finally so aware of all your imperfections, let's start working on them, starting with your awful appearance!"

Stinkin' discouragement thinkin' quickly steps in. "I have been telling you all along you should not think so highly of yourself. Now that you are knocked down to size, welcome to the barely tolerable existence of the human race. You are stuck in misery."

Stinkin' lust thinkin' slithers in and says, "Well, you can no longer have the satisfaction of thinking you are better than others. There is a better satisfaction than that, and I will lead you to it. Let's go get some action."

Stinkin' depression thinkin' rises up and says, "Have you ever considered whether your life is even worth the effort anymore?"

Stinkin' envy thinkin' brews in the brain. "Look at how successful and happy everyone else is. Too bad for you, huh?"

Finally *stinkin' anger thinkin'* blows your brains, and you exclaim, to no one there, "I am not going to put up with anything from anyone. Just mess with me, and see what you get!"

One demon is removed, and seven demons fill the vacuum.[3]

> *To the Victor belong all the spoils.*

When a stronghold is removed, even during the removal process you should already be filling your mind with Scripture, praise worship songs, the nature of God, sacred memories, conversations

---

3. Though true believers cannot be possessed by demons, we can be mesmerized and troubled by mental strongholds originating from Satan's deception. As pastor, I have encountered many church members who, though they claim to be Christ followers, were no doubt controlled by the enemy. Having churchianity is not the same as being in Christ. For anyone, the first step toward mental wellness is surrender of all of self-life, thoughts, relationships, motives, etc. to the Lordship of Christ.

with a mentor, love, joy, peace, patience, kindness, goodness, faithfulness, gentleness, and self-control. Let the Spirit of Christ dwell richly and fully within your heart and mind, and you will realize that you are complete in Christ, mature in the inner man.

PRINCIPLE SEVEN: GIVE THE SPOILS TO THE VICTOR

> Do not take any of the things set apart
> for destruction, or you yourselves will be
> completely destroyed, and you will bring
> trouble on the camp of Israel.
> Everything made from silver, gold, bronze, or iron
> is sacred to the LORD
> and must be brought into his treasury.
> (Josh 6:18–19 NLT)

Since God gave his people the victory, all the loot belonged to him. The people were to bring all the valuables into God's house, holding nothing back from him. All the spoils belonged to the Victor. God gave clear instructions of the danger of taking what belonged to him.

Who owns your life? To whom do you belong? When it comes to your resources, time, relationships, and possessions, do you act more like an owner, or like a manager? Are there things that belong to God that you hold onto as if they are yours? Do you sometimes credit yourself for what God has done? When he gives you victory, do you give him the spoils?

Do you ever hold back giving tithes at church because you don't like certain things about the church? Do you have joy and gladness over the victories God has given to you or do you speak in criticism and faithlessness?

If there is any victory in your life, if there are financial advances made through the years, if there is any accumulation of wealth, God is the One who has brought it all into reality. He is the One who gives you the power to make wealth (Deut 8:18). He is the One who conquers your strongholds so you can enjoy victorious life in Christ. To the victor belong the spoils.

When God breaks down a stronghold in your life, give him all the glory, all the praise, all the spoils, and all of yourself!

Principles for Overcoming Strongholds

PRINCIPLE EIGHT: REACH OUT TO UNBELIEVERS WHO WILL BELIEVE

> "Meanwhile," Joshua said to the two spies,
> "Keep your promise. Go to the prostitute's house
> and bring her out, along with all her family."
> (Josh 6:22 NLT)

Weeks prior to the people of God approaching Jericho, Joshua sent out two spies to Jericho to scout out the land around it. The men came to the house of Rahab, a prostitute.

Someone told the king that two spies were in the city at Rahab's house. Soldiers came asking Rahab for the spies, but Rahab hid them. Since her house was built into the city wall, she let the spies escape the city by going down a rope hung out her window.

Before they left Rahab, the men promised her they would spare her and her family when they came back to conquer the city. Joshua reminded these two men of their promise, and they saved Rahab and her family from death.

When God conquers a stronghold, he not only does it for the sake of his own people, he also uses the victory to draw others toward faith in him. God takes those we would not consider worthy, and draws them into his royal family.

Hebrews chapter 11, the great hall of faith, includes Rahab's name. Rahab evidently later married into a Jewish family, because she is listed in the genealogy of Jesus himself!

Imagine being Rahab. You live in a house within the city wall, and have watched out your window as the people of God march around your city once every day for six days. You hear the eerie blowing of ram's horns. It becomes routine viewing, until on the seventh day you see them march seven times around.

Suddenly the crowd of a million or more people shout at the top of their lungs. The trumpets blast like never before. Together with the marching feet, it creates an earthquake of 8.2 on the Richter scale. You run to the other side of your house, and look out the window toward the inside of fort Jericho. You see the walls of all four sides of the fort beginning to crumble. You thank God that he has given you undeserved favor, as the two spies you helped weeks ago come running to your house and sweep you and your children away to safety. You, Rahab, are saved by God's grace through your faith

When God breaks down strongholds in our lives, he often intentionally allows Rahab kinds of people to be a part of it. Curious people, whom we would have never been voted "most likely to become a Christian," will take note of the great work of God in bringing down the stronghold. They will stand amazed at something incredible happening. They may even ask you, "What in the world is going on?"

God tears down our strongholds to catch the attention of people like Rahab so that he can save them. When God brings down a stronghold for you, brag on him to those who have yet to believe. See what God does to reach people through you.

There is one requirement for reaching your Rahabs. Are you willing to be transparent with others about the battles you are facing, and both the victories and setbacks you experience?

Are you stuck in some kind of mental rut? Is there a stronghold in your heart and mind that needs to come down? Does something have a hold on you, and you just can't seem to break free from it?

- Believe that God has given the victory already!
- Accept a new plan without resistance.
- Silence the voice of unbelief.
- Keep obeying, even when it seems foolish!
- Shout about the victory before it comes!
- Curse the rebuilding of the stronghold.
- Give the spoils to the victor.
- Reach out to unbelievers who will believe.

PRINCIPLES FOR OVERCOMING STRONGHOLDS

Questions for Reflection and Discussion

1. Read Joshua 6:1–2. What is your Jericho? What stronghold(s) do you face? Are things like shame, anger, lust, inferiority, pride, addiction, or depression a part of your life?

2. Read Joshua 6:3–6. We become the plan we follow. From what source do your plans originate? Do you make your own plans?

3. Do you create your plans based on providing security for yourself, assuring that things will stay the same for you?

   Have you considered that God is on the move, and if you are to be in step with him, you must stop following your own plans, which may keep you stuck in the mud, and accept his plan without resistance?

4. Read Joshua 6:10. Are there voices saying things to you which are *not* based on faith in God? Have you ever considered that it is possible to silence the voice of unbelief?

   Are there marching orders that God has given you, and yet instead of marching obediently, you let the voices of unbelief in your head argue with God about those marching orders?

   When God said, "March," did you say, "Yes, Lord," and start to march, however while marching, you tried to reason with God to change the marching orders?

How easy is it for you to practice the spiritual discipline of silence?

Go to a place of guaranteed solitude with only the clothing you are wearing—no pen, no watch no paper, no phone, no Bible. Practice half a day of silence.

5. Read Joshua 6:11, 14. Have you been faithful with the day-by-day march?

If a stronghold is persisting, pray now, asking God what his "day seven" radical action is to make your Jericho come a tumblin' down. Wait for his answer. Write his plan here, then do what he says:

6. Read Joshua 6:15–16. What gets you shouting?

What needs to happen to your faith so that you can shout about promised victories before you even see them?

7. Read Joshua 6:17, 26. Ever try to rid yourself of something ungodly, only to find that you have become even more ungodly?

What should you do to fill up the vacuum left by sin's removal?

8. Read Joshua 6:18–19. Who owns your life? To whom do you belong?

Principles for Overcoming Strongholds

When it comes to your resources, time, relationships, and possessions, do you act more like an owner, or like a manager?

Are there things that belong to God that you hold on to as if they are yours?

Do you sometimes credit yourself for what God has done?

When he gives you victory, do you give him the spoils?

9. Read Joshua 6:18–19. Has God placed unbelievers in your path to see the work he is doing in your life? Who are they?

   Are you willing to be transparent with others about the battles you are facing, and both the victories and setbacks you experience?

10. For a great study of spiritual victory through the cross of Christ, examine the following verses and write down principles gleamed from them:

    1 Corinthians 15:57

    2 Corinthians 5:17–18

    Romans 6:14

Whoopin' Up on Stinkin' Thinkin'

Romans 8:11

Romans 8:37

Hebrews 7:25–27

Colossians 2:15

Galatians 2:20

1 Peter 3:18–22

Revelation 12:11

*Trust in the Lord
with all your heart;
do not lean on
your own understanding.*

Proverbs 3:5 NLT

9

Temptation Stinks!

IF THE SON SETS you free, you are free indeed! There is no condemnation for those who are in Christ Jesus. However, your freedom in Christ can be abused. Satan will plant subtle thoughts in your mind to lure you into temptation's traps.

"I'm deprived of life's basic essentials. I'm not getting enough of the good stuff." *Stinkin' thinkin'*.

"I see with my eyes how the world is full of things I don't have, yet other people have all they want." *Stinkin' thinkin'*.

"By working hard for a long time, and gaining so much by my own efforts, I have proven to the world my own worth." *Stinkin' thinkin'*.

What is temptation? How can you know when you are tempted and when you are not tempted? Is being tempted the same as sinning? How can you have victory over temptation?

Temptation is Satan enticing you to act independently of God. Satan makes sin look fun, and let's face it; sin *is* fun . . . for a little while. However, after a while, sin starts to ruin us.

> *You can't stop a bird from flying over your head, but you can keep it from building a nest in your hair.*

It is not a sin to be tempted. Jesus was tempted, yet he had no sin. It is a sin to *give in* to temptation. You can't keep a bird from flying over your head. However, you can keep it from building a nest in your hair! You may have a wayward thought that seeks to draw you into sin. That thought in itself is not sinful, but you don't have to let that thought linger. Take it captive as a prisoner of spiritual warfare. Lingering on a tempting thought *is* sinful.

Often the tempting thought is so attractive that we don't see it as sinful. We see it as good. We slowly become sympathetic with the pleas of the voice speaking to us, and before you know it we are won over to the wrong side of the battle for our brains.

On August 23, 1973, Erik Olson, out of prison on parole, attempted to hold up a bank in Stockholm, Sweden. Police showed up. Erik took four hostages and held them for a six-day standoff.

It's bazaar but true; Erik managed to convince his captives that they were safe with him, but not with the police. The hostages refused rescue attempts. Later, they even refused to testify against their captor. Those who had been held captive even raised money for the defense of their captor! Now, whenever a similar situation occurs, it is referred to as the "Stockholm Syndrome."

The enemy's clever deceptions cause our thinking to get all turned around. We begin to think those who promote evil are the good, fun guys. Those who stand for good are the unwanted, bad guys. Satan takes our minds captive and convinces us he's the good guy offering us the best life possible.

He convinces us with so-called common sense, saying, "It's only natural to fulfill your body's cravings. If you are hungry, you should eat. If you crave sex, you should go find a willing body." *Stinkin' thinkin'*.

"If you see something you like, of course you should not deprive yourself of it." *Stinkin' thinkin'*.

"The only thing you can depend on is you, yourself." *Stinkin' thinkin'*.

> For the world offers
> only a craving for physical pleasure,
> a craving for everything we see,
> and pride in our achievements and possessions.
> (1 John 2:16)

Notice three sources of temptation; the flesh, the eyes, and the heart. Examine your thoughts to see if you have fallen into the tempting traps of craving physical pleasure (the flesh), desiring to have what you see (the eyes), and trusting self for security (the heart).

Here's the *stinkin' thinkin'* mental process:

Whoopin' Up on Stinkin' Thinkin'

I feel empty. I crave.
I feel deprived. I lust.
I feel rejected. I boast to feel worth.

In the Bible, there is an intriguing and helpful comparison between two "Adams." The first Adam fell for the three areas of temptation (Gen 2–3), while Jesus, who is called the last Adam (1 Cor 15:21–22, 45–48), was tempted in the same three areas yet did not give in (Matt 4; Luke 4). Before we examine these things in detail, it is helpful to see it in chart form.

Tempting Traps	The First Adam's Failure Gen 3	The Last Adam's Victory Luke 4; Matt 4
Lust: Where is my passion?	Fulfilling basic urges outside of God's plan.	Depending on the Father for life.
Coveting: Where is my vision?	Seeing self served whatever self sees.	Seeing God alone worshipped and served.
Pride: What gives me "worth"?	Proving my own value to others.	Refusing to ask God to prove anything: Letting God be God.

> The first man, Adam, became a living person.
> But the last Adam—that is, Christ—is a life-giving Spirit.
> What comes first is the natural body,
> then the spiritual body comes later.
> Adam, the first man, was made from
> the dust of the earth,
> while Christ, the second man, came from heaven.
> Earthly people are like the earthly man,
> and heavenly people are like the heavenly man.
> (1 Cor 15:45–48)

Our first birth gives us physical life. Those who have only been born physically have no choice but to follow the urges of the body. However, a second birth is possible.

> Just as everyone dies because we all belong to Adam,
> everyone who belongs to Christ will be given new life.
> (1 Cor 15:22)

Through faith in Christ a person can be born again. At this second birth, you receive spiritual life through Christ's Spirit coming to live in you, empowering you to ignore the impulse of the flesh and instead follow the imprint of the Spirit within your heart.

TEMPTING TRAP ONE

Lust: Where Is Your Passion?

> For the world offers
> only a craving for physical pleasure . . .
> (1 John 2:16)

The Greek word "craving" is *epithumia*, which means desire, or passion. Where is *your* passion? Are your more passionate about your body's appearance and pleasures than you are passionate about your spirit's health and nurturing? If we expect to win the spiritual battle over lust, our passion for dependence on God's provision for our basic needs must exceed our carnal passion to have our needs met.

Where is your passion? Do you spend much of your days thinking about how you will get your physical desires met? Or do you thirst for God like someone having spent days in a dry desert (Ps 63:1; 34:8)?

In the Bible, though *epithumia* is a morally neutral term, it most often refers to a basic animalistic urge within humans that very easily gets out of control. It is the lust of the flesh. The "flesh" is our basic, lower, biological nature.

How do you know if you have given in to the lust of the flesh? Remember, even the most basic desires within us were put there by God. He has not only given us the desires, he has also given us appropriate ways to have those desires met. The deceiver comes along and offers to meet those desires in illegitimate ways that are very attractive, yet harmful to us in the end.

When determining if you have given in to the lust of the flesh, here is a question to ask yourself before God: *God, am I meeting my own physical needs outside of your provision? If so, I am being carnal. Show me your*

Whoopin' Up on Stinkin' Thinkin'

provision for my need and help me wait. If you ask God to provide, and wait for his provision, you are being spiritual.

If you let physical desires control your body, you allow a mental stronghold to wrap itself around your mind like a python snake, resulting in self-destructive behaviors such as gluttony, drunkenness, and sexual immorality. You will become much like a mere animal.

Maybe it seems to you like you are far too spiritual to let such a thing happen. You may be in a sweet spot in your relationship with God, walking in the garden area of true soul connection with him. Adam and Eve were in such a garden as well, until one day the tempter came along, confusing their thoughts.

> "Did God really say you must not eat the fruit from any of the trees in the garden?"
> "Of course we may eat fruit from the trees in the garden," the woman replied. "It's only the fruit from the tree in the middle of the garden that we are not allowed to eat. God said, 'You must not eat it or even touch it; if you do, you will die.'"
> "You won't die!" the serpent replied to the woman.
> (Gen 3:1–4)

Satan planted *stinkin' thinkin'* in Eve's mind. "Did God really say you can't eat of *all* the trees?" He insinuated that God was holding back all of his goodness.

How quickly Eve started agreeing with her captor! "He even said we can't *touch* that fruit!" That was not true. God had not said that. Eve was just joining in on Satan's God-bashing. "You are right, Satan. God is not only withholding good food from us, he won't even let us touch it!"

The first humans were deceived into believing they would be better off taking care of their own desires instead of letting God provide for them by his plan. The first Adam failed. Though desire for food is a legitimate, God-given desire, the choice was made to fulfill that desire outside of God's plan.

Jesus, the "last Adam," was tempted in the same way. However, unlike the first Adam, who failed by fulfilling basic urges outside of God's plan, the last Adam experienced victory by depending on the Father for life.

> Then Jesus was led by the Spirit into the wilderness to be tempted there by the devil.

> For forty days and forty nights
> he fasted and became very hungry.
> During that time the devil came and said to him,
> "If you are the Son of God,
> tell these stones to become loaves of bread."
> But Jesus told him, "No! The Scriptures say,
> 'People do not live by bread alone, but by
> every word that comes from the mouth of God.'"
> (Matt 4:1–4)

The enemy knows just when to attack. Temptation is greatest when you are hungry, tired, all alone, and especially when you have purposefully gone to a place to connect with the Father in solitude.

Satan comes along and says, *In this miserable place, if you don't do something good for yourself, you are showing just how wimpy and small you really are. Don't you have what it takes to even meet your own basic needs? Go out and get it, man!*

God creates us with certain desires, but Satan tempts us to fulfill those desires in evil ways, which turns desire into lust.

God made us to need food. We should eat to live, but instead we live to eat! The result is a mental stronghold that says, "Whenever I am feeling anxiety, I will turn to food for some feel-good relief." *Stinkin' thinkin'*.

There's nothing sinful about eating, yet we eat when we're not even hungry! There are limits to *what* we should eat, and *how much* we should eat. Don't allow a passion for food to be what drives you.

Jesus fasted for forty days, and even then, at that point of hunger, was able to have victory over food temptation! What if you and I were to try fasting as a spiritual discipline to gain victory over stomach strongholds?

God made us to need shelter. However, in America it's so easy to agree with the deceiver, and say, "My worth is shown by the size and style of my accommodations." *Stinkin' thinkin'*. Such a mental stronghold results in selling self both to the bondage of debt and to the fickle opinions of others.

Rest is a God-given need. However, we in America have turned recreational pursuits into a huge, costly, stressful industry. As parents, we may feel peer pressure to think, "If we don't have our kids join the weekend family sports travel team, our children will be emotionally scarred for life!" *Stinkin' thinkin'*.

Whoopin' Up on Stinkin' Thinkin'

Being on a sports team can be a great experience, but only if you are doing it because it is good for your family. Whatever happened to the simple forms of recreation like playing together outside in the yard, enjoying horseshoes, having a campfire, and taking a family walk in the woods?

Sex is a God-given need. However, God's design is the fulfillment of our sexual appetite within the sacredness of marriage. If we indulge in sex in other directions, such as sex outside of marriage, homosexuality, or self-centered sex, the result will be bondage.

The secret to sexual purity is in the way you think. The only way to control your sex life is to control your thoughts. Jesus said, "Anyone who even looks at a woman with lust has already committed adultery with her in his heart" (Matt 5:28).

The moment your eyes see someone who catches your attention, you are still without sin, if you immediately look away. However, if you let your eyes linger, sin is in your heart already. Change what you are looking at and what you are thinking about. Move on.

Avoid tempting trap #1 by asking yourself, *Where is my passion?* Develop a passion for God and for his provision of all you need.

TEMPTING TRAP TWO

Coveting: Where Is Your Vision?

> For the world offers only . . .
> a craving for everything we see . . .
> (1 John 2:16)

The word "see" is the Greek word *ophthalaemon*, from which we get our word ophthalmology. Where is your vision? Is it time for an optometric exam? We are easily captivated by external appearances, instead of being guided by an unseen yet very real vision of life's preferred direction.

When the lust of the eyes guides life, trouble results. Cheryl and I watched the Netflix series *The Durrells of Corfu*, in which the son becomes old enough to live on his own. He moves into a simple apartment, where he discovers the female landlord is not only quite attractive, she finds him irresistible.

What starts out feeling like wonderfully crazy love, ends up with the landlord becoming completely overbearing with demands on not only

Temptation Stinks!

the young man, but his entire family. Fed up, the young man comes to his senses, moves out, and breaks it off with his former landlord.

The first Adam and Eve were enticed by Satan into sin through their eyes.

> The woman was convinced.
> She saw that the tree was beautiful;
> its fruit looked delicious . . .
> (Gen 3:6)

Like the first Adam, we covet. Our vision is on the wrong things. We see to it that self is served whatever self sees. Satan has deceived us into thinking, "I can ignore God, serve myself, and still not die!" *Stinkin' thinkin'*.

Jesus, the last Adam, was also tempted to covet what he saw. However, he experienced victory over temptation because his vision was on worshipping and serving the Father, not self.

> Then the devil took him up and revealed to him
> all the kingdoms of the world in a moment of time.
> "I will give you the glory of these kingdoms and authority over them,"
> the devil said,
> "because they are mine to give to anyone I please.
> I will give it all to you if you worship me."
> Jesus replied, "The Scriptures say,
> 'You must worship the Lord your God
> and serve him only.'"
> (Luke 4:5–8)

Satan has supernatural ability, though limited. He was able to reveal to Jesus, in one moment's time, the entire realm of evil spiritual authority over all the earthly kingdoms of the entire planet. It is true that Satan has some temporary authority over this earth. However, this is still our Father's world, and one day soon he will make that very clear! Satan was no doubt trying to impress Jesus, which is the same tactic he seeks to use on you and me.

I find it interesting that Jesus did not try to straighten out the devil's twisting thinking. If I were Jesus in that moment, I might have argued with the devil, saying, "This world is not yours to give, you lying chump! All the authority has been given to *me*, not you." However, Jesus simply quoted Scripture and refused to argue with the devil.

The deceiver wants to make us think his power controls the world, that everything belongs to him, and that without him we have nothing. He makes himself sound like our savior, offering us the whole world. He plants such thoughts in our minds, and we start saying to self, *Oh my! See all that the world has to offer! It could all be mine!*

In that moment, we decide one of two things. The most typical decision is to agree with what we have told ourselves. *I must begin to live as if this world is all there is, because it is so. My best course in life is to follow my inner impulses and do whatever seems right to self.* In the end, however, we find ourselves, empty, unfulfilled, and self-destructing from Satan's deception.

A second option *is* available. We can remind ourselves of the truth. God owns everything in this world, not Satan. We recognize that Satan seeks to steal and kill and destroy by coaxing us into living for ourselves instead of God. We choose not to serve self by not coveting the things we see in this world. Instead, our vision is on seeing God alone worshipped and served.

> *We buy things we don't need, with money we don't have, to keep up with people we don't even like.*

Joe Gutierrez was a steelworker. At forty-one years of age, he recalls silvery dust falling through the air at the plant. It looked so beautiful, workers and guests would gather to see the glittery glow at night, and let it cover them, as if it were some kind of magical snow. The dust they so admired turned out to be . . . *asbestos*! Oh the things we see; enchanting to the eye, but deadly.

Coveting takes on so many different forms. Desiring physical things we see is the most basic form of coveting. God made us to possess things, but they end up possessing us! We buy things we don't need, with money we don't have, to keep up with people we don't even like!

I need a better car to feel good about myself. Everybody else is driving a new car. Stinkin' thinkin'. The truth is everyone drives a used car. It became used the moment it was driven off the car lot. The truth is your self-worth is not derived from the car you drive but from whose you are, and from who you are in Christ.

If you envy others that have more possessions than you do, then coveting is a stronghold for you. Is your vision on the material, instead of the ultimate spiritual realm of life?

Another form of coveting is desiring a person in a way you should not.

King David probably should have been out with his men in battle. Instead, he was up on his roof enjoying the day. He saw Bathsheba sunbathing. He could have immediately looked away, gone inside, and switched his mind to something else.

Instead, he kept looking, and used his power as the king to have another man's wife. He was captivated by external appearances. He even had Bathsheba's husband sent to the front line of battle so he would die.

The prophet Nathan rebuked David, and David confessed and repented, admitting his guilt before God and others. Though the child of David and Bathsheba died, David stayed close with God and worshipped him, having learned a fatal lesson about the lust of the eyes. From then on, David no longer coveted whatever he saw. Instead, he kept his vision on seeing God alone worshipped and served.

Coveting a person you should not have as your own can also take place in the virtual world. God made our eyes to enjoy beauty. We have, however, turned it into pornography. Instead of indulging in virtual fantasies, we should each live by the prayer found in Psalm 119:37. *Turn my eyes from worthless things, and give me life through your word.*

There is yet another form of coveting that is so subtle, it goes largely unnoticed. This kind of coveting is extremely common among followers of Christ. It is coveting the blessings of God more than loving God himself.

Christ says that you as his follower are his bride. He is the groom. The groom showers you, his bride, with crazy love. If you are not careful, you can start to enjoy the wedding gifts more than the marriage, as if you were some engaged woman who shows off the ring more than the man.

Even as a Christ follower, it is possible to have misplaced vision, loving the benefits of being a Christ follower more than Christ himself. Where is your vision? Consider your spiritual experience in terms of how you talk about it. "Oh, I absolutely love the fellowship. I love the Bible studies. I love the sun coming through the stained glass the way it does, and those worship songs really get me going." Where is Christ in all that? Sometimes we make "worship" all about us.

Do you love him, or do you merely love the trappings in which you find him? Are you captivated by what you see and feel and experience at church, or are you captivated by Christ? Where is your vision?

If you merely desire an experience you can see and feel, you will never have enough. You will always seek to see something greater, and feel something even deeper, which may lead you to drop out of church when you don't hit the next expected high. However, if you do not desire to see or feel or know anything but *Christ* himself, you will never be disappointed. Where is your vision?

Avoid the second trap of temptation. Refuse to covet what you see, whether what you see is a thing, a person, or an experience. Desire to see God alone worshipped and served. Do you rely more on your own perspective, or on God's perspective? Where is your vision?

TEMPTING TRAP THREE

Pride: What Gives You "Worth"?

> For the world offers only . . .
> pride in our achievements and possessions.
> (1 John 2:16)

The word "pride" is *alazoneia*, a Greek word which was often used to describe a quack who traveled around emptily boasting of having cures for people's ills. Biblically, *alaozoneia* describes a boastful, arrogant person who puts an empty trust in the stability of earthly things, as is displayed in his or her style of living. It also describes someone who is pretending to be someone he or she isn't; pretending to be more important, more experienced, or wealthier than is actually true.

I have personally struggled with some *stinkin' thinkin'* in this area, so I ask myself some tough questions. Though I am about to let you in on my private conversation with myself, I'd appreciate it if doesn't go any farther than just between you and me. Let's just keep it right here between us. If other people knew about it, it might hurt my pride.

Do I live by human ambition?

Do I strive in my own strength to reach goals I have set for myself? If so, what difference, if any, is there between me and someone who does not profess to follow Christ? Are the goals that I hold dearly things that I have waited for Christ to reveal to me, and if not, then do I deceive myself into thinking I am 100 percent God-directed? When I brag on the spiritual victories occurring within the body of Christ I shepherd, what part does my own human ambition play in that bragging?

Do I desire to outshine others?

Is life, for me, one big competition? Do I listen to the stories of other people only so that I can top that story with my own bigger story? Do I go to a pastor's meeting desiring to find out which pastors there have churches larger or smaller than the one I pastor? Have I allowed Satan to deceive me into exaggerating God's command to "have dominion over the earth" (Gen 1:26–28)?

Do I try to impress others that I am more than I actually am?

Do I think my sense of worth depends on what others think of me? Can I not be content in simply knowing that I am his and he is mine? Why does my sense of worth have to ride on my performance? I think I am depending on Christ, but when the rug is pulled out from underneath me, I find out just how much I depend on myself and my own ability to produce. Why do I feel like I must prove myself to others?

God, reduce me to the point of having nothing to prove. I don't want my life to be about me. I want to let you be God. Life, yes, my life, is to be all about you. Help it be so.

Having looked at my own *stinkin' thinkin'*, I am now quite ready to examine someone else's faults! Let's take a final look at the first Adam.

The first Adam's prideful failure was in wanting to be as God. Adam did not want to be *godly*. He wanted to be a *god* himself. Satan convinced him that he could and should an equal with God. He also insinuated that if Adam did not go after godlike power, Adam would merely be a puppet, strung onto God's fingers.

> God knows that your eyes will be opened
> as soon as you eat it, and you will be like God,
> knowing both good and evil.
> (Gen 3:5)

I can just imagine Adam's mental wheels starting to turn. *Hmm . . . Think about it! Me . . . having what God is withholding from me . . . my eyes wide open . . . knowing all there is to know just like God knows . . . instead of being a mere puppet, I get to be the puppeteer of the universe, just like God! Wow! All this waiting for me inside this little piece of fruit! What a great way to show my true worth to everyone. Gotta bite into all that right now!*

And so, Adam bit into all that. And you and I continue to bite into it as well. We thirst for applause, honor, power, and recognition from what we have made of ourselves. We will only stop striving once we feel we have

Whoopin' Up on Stinkin' Thinkin'

sufficiently been recognized for the great worth we supposedly possess. Is there no escape from the pride trap we have inherited from the first Adam?

The Last Adam gained victory over pride by refusing to prove himself to anyone. We turn again to the account of Jesus' response to Satan's wilderness tempting, this time seeing it from Matthew' perspective:

> Then the devil took him to the holy city,
> Jerusalem, to the highest point of the Temple,
> and said, "If you are the Son of God, jump off!
> For the Scriptures say, 'He will order his angels to protect you.
> And they will hold you up with their hands
> so you won't even hurt your foot on a stone.'"
> Jesus responded, "The scriptures also say,
> 'You must not test the Lord your God.'"
> (Matt 4:5–7)

Jesus refused to play Satan's "prove it to the world" game. Jesus reminded Satan that we should not make God prove himself to us. If God has nothing to prove, why should we have something to prove? Life is not about me. It's not about you. Don't live under Satan's deception that you have to prove your worth. You don't have to show off your greatness by jumping off the church steeple!

What is the way of escape from Satan's tricky temptations? We must examine the way we think, take every loose thought captive, and make it obey Christ.

When you do so, here's what happens: Temptation still knocks on the door of your heart, still seeking to lure you into some *stinkin' thinkin'*. However, instead of answering the door yourself, you send Jesus to the door. The devil senses the power of Jesus coming, and doesn't even wait for Jesus to open the door. Satan just runs and hides as quickly as he can.

> The temptations in your life are
> no different from what others experience.
> And God is faithful. He will not allow
> the temptation to be more than you can stand.
> When you are tempted,
> he will show you a way out
> so that you can endure.
> (1 Cor 10:13)

Temptation Stinks!

Praying God's word back to him can be very helpful in overcoming temptation.

Lord, I crave physical pleasure. Right now, I have the opportunity to fulfill the lust within me. You promise in 1 Corinthians 10:13 that you will show me a way out. Where is it, God? Show me the way out now. I choose to take that way out. Help me not to live by physical things but, as Jesus did in Matthew 4:4, by every word that comes from your mouth.

Oh, God, how I crave the things I see around me in this world. It seems like I deceive myself into thinking that life is only about the world I see around me. I pray that you would, as Psalm 119:37 says, turn my eyes from worthless things, and give me life through your word. Help me see your eternal, heavenly realm, and live with eternity in view.

My Father, most people around me are naturally proud of their achievements and possessions. I have become that way myself. Forgive me. I put no more trust in the stability of earthly things or in my ability to provide for myself and my family. Change my heart, oh, God. Though I love my family, they are undeserved gifts from you, not the results of my own goodness. Help me to realize moment by moment that 1 John 2:16 is true; the pride of life comes not from you Father but from the world around me. I take every prideful thought captive and make it obey Christ. Remove any and all sense of self-achievement from my heart.

Whoopin' Up on Stinkin' Thinkin'

TEMPTATION STINKS!

Questions for Reflection and Discussion

1. Which, if any, do you often think?

    ____ "My physical desires are not being met." (Lust of the flesh)

    ____ "There are so many things I see that I really want." (Lust of the eyes)

    ____ "I must make sure everyone knows my achievements, my good qualities, and my true worth." (Pride of life)

2. Memorize 1 Corinthians 10:13 and ask God to help you apply it to one specific temptation you are facing. Share with a trusted friend, asking for accountability.

3. Read Jesus' victory over temptation in Matthew 4 and Luke 4.

    What principles did Jesus use in having victory over temptation?

-
-
-
-

4. Go to an online source such as biblehub.com and look at 1 John 2:16. Click on the "parallel" tab to read the verse in several different translations. Define . . .

    Lust of the flesh

Lust of the eyes

Pride of life

5. In what ways do you sometimes seek to fulfill your basic urges outside of God's plan?

6. In what ways do you serve self instead of worshipping and serving God alone?

7. Are there any ways in which you love your religious experience more than you love Christ himself?

8. What gives you a sense of worth?

9. Memorize 1 John 2:16 from whatever translation you choose. Reflect on what God says through your time meditating on the verse:

10. Study the Scripture a bit more broadly on the subject of temptation. Write your own prayers, praying God's word back to him:

*Think about the things
of heaven,
not the things of earth.
For you died to this life,
and your real life
is hidden with Christ in God.*

Colossians 3:2–3 NLT

10

The Ultimate Whoopin'!

BRENDAN SCHWEIGART WAS WEARING a bulletproof vest during a critical mission in Baghdad, Iraq. He was a twenty-two-year-old Private First Class in the Army. Before he went out to the battleground, he tucked his Bible down into a pocket inside his vest.

The mission turned dangerous. A powerful bullet penetrated the shield and was heading for Brendan's heart, when it was stopped by the Bible. Days later when Brendan was released from the hospital, he showed people the bullet, still lodged in the pages of his Bible. [1]

Do you allow your thoughts and desires to be shaped by Scripture?

The Bible protected him when the shield did not! While physical weapons fail us, the spiritual power of the Word of God protects us from the attacks of the enemy!

There is a battle for our minds. We must carry God's word with us into life's daily battles. We must hide God's word in our heart. In those times when we do not have the mind of Christ, when we have slipped into stinkin' thinkin', we should turn to the Bible, asking God to guide us to truth in his word that will correct our thinking. And then we should pray God's word back to him. In doing so, we will be saved from the enemy's attack.

1. facebook.com/BibleDailyDevotionalPrayer/posts/pfc-brendan-schweigart

Whoopin' Up on Stinkin' Thinkin'

> All scripture is inspired by God
> and is useful to teach us what is true
> and to make us realize what is wrong in our lives.
> It corrects us when we are wrong
> and teaches us to do what is right.
> (2 Tim 3:16)

When you pray God's word back to him, he reminds you what is true, so that you can think on truth, not deception. When you pray God's word, he points out to you what is wrong with your way of thinking. Praying God's word transforms your mind like nothing else. If you are ready to give your stinkin' thinkin' the ultimate whoopin,' pray God's word.

There is a condition which God places on his willingness to partner with you in breaking down the strongholds of your mind.

> If you remain in me
> and my words remain in you,
> you may ask for anything you want,
> and it will be granted.
> (John 15:7 NLT)

As a pastor, I have noticed through the years just how possible it is for us as believers to memorize and recite God's Word yet all the while never allowing those very words to mold the way we think. When it comes to God's word...

We memorize without meditating.
We receive without reacting.
We articulate without applying.

The words of Scripture cognitively enter our brain's memory banks, yet we do not consider how we need to be changed by those words. We pride ourselves in piling up Scripture knowledge while our lives do not change. Regardless of how many years we have achieved perfect Sunday School attendance, God is evaluating us on whether we *obey* him. A disciple, according to Jesus, is *one who obeys*.

Christ's words must abide fully in each compartment of your thought life. To develop the mind of Christ, you must free up every area of your thinking to be filled with the thoughts that Christ himself would think. God answers your prayer for mental transformation only to the degree you allow your mind and your life to be shaped by Scripture.

The Ultimate Whoopin'!

In 1990, after starting churches in Texas, Cheryl and I, along with four-year-old Joshua and eleven-month-old Jonathan, transplanted our lives to Korea. We spent the first two years of missionary service in full-time language study.

There in Korea, the strongholds of pride, ethnocentrism, and anger began digging roots in my mind. I was aware of these strongholds taking hold in my inner man, yet I felt that, due to my severe challenges in life, I needed and deserved these mental crutches.

They told us Korean is one of the most difficult languages to learn. They lied to us. It is not one of the most difficult. It is *the* most difficult language! To burn off the stress of language study, I played tennis most every day. Though I usually played with young men around my same age, one day a group of grandfathers asked me to play with them.

I began wondering what it would be like, in a country where hierarchical structure governs all of life, to play tennis with those who reside on the top rung of society. As soon as I set foot on the court, I began to find out!

"Listen up, young man. When you play tennis with a Korean grandpa, don't hit the ball where the grandpa isn't. Hit the ball straight to him. And when you hit the ball, don't hit it too fast. You serve first."

Just as I was tossing up the ball to serve, the grandpas scolded me. "Don't you know anything? Where did you come from anyway? Before you serve the ball to a grandpa, you must bow before him." So from that point, before every serve, I performed a deep, solemn, ceremonial bow to each and every grandpa. The grandpas laughed at me each time. Little did I know that only one initial bow on only the first serve of the match was all that was required.

I could feel my anger starting to develop. The littlest thing might set me off. At that point, one of the grandfathers must have thought he was playing baseball. He hit a home run over the fence and across a six-lane road.

It was like the entire world stood still. None of the grandfathers, not even those who had come out just to see the fun that was being had at the expense of a young American, said one single word. They all stopped and stared at me. With their eyes, they said, "Go get the ball."

At that point, my ethnocentrism wanted to say, "In America, he who hits the ball goes to get the ball. Go get the ball, Grandpa." *Stinkin' thinkin'*.

Whoopin' Up on Stinkin' Thinkin'

My pride wanted to say, "You think you are so important, don't you! And who do you think I am? An errand boy?" *Stinkin' thinkin'*.

My anger wanted to say, "I am sick and tired of you guys making fun of me. I'm done. Goodbye forever!" *Stinkin' thinkin'*.

At least I was smart enough to keep my mouth shut! So, I went to get the ball, venting all of those pent-up thoughts to myself. Suddenly, seemingly out of nowhere, 1 Corinthians 9:22 came to mind. *I have become all things to all people so that by all means I might win some*. I wasn't done having my temper tantrum yet, so I ignored the verse and completed my fetching assignment.

I went back to the court to bow some more and be laughed at some more. Then another grandpa hit *his* home run! As I went to fetch once again, I said to myself, *Who do they think I am, a ball-fetching dog?* However, once again, the phrase came to mind; *I become all things to all people so that by all means I might win some*.

Finally, I let God in on my thoughts. "God, these grandpas think I'm a slave. They are laughing at me." God then troubled me by showing me my own pride, as clearly as if he had put up a mirror in front of my heart.

I finally surrendered to what he was trying to teach me, and said, *Alright, God. First Corinthians 9:22 says I am to become all things to all people so that by all means I might win some to Christ. I am willing to become an errand boy for these Korean old men so that I might win some Koreans to Christ. Just help change my attitude, please!*

God did change my heart. It wasn't long before one of my tennis partners, Haeji's father, noticed the change and gave his life to Christ! Praying God's word back to him can change your life, make you able to bear spiritual fruit, and bring others into the kingdom.

Remember, a stronghold is a prevailing thought pattern that takes root in your mind, mixing truth with deceptive lies, designed by the enemy to put you, God's child, into bondage. The stronghold sets itself up as a lofty thought, keeping you from experiencing God. We are to use spiritual weapons with divine power to knock down strongholds and take captive every thought for Christ (2 Cor 10:3–5). The Word of God is a mighty weapon for whoopin' up on stinkin' thinkin'.

> For the word of God is alive and powerful.
> It is sharper than the sharpest two-edged sword,
> cutting between soul and spirit,

The Ultimate Whoopin'!

> between joint and marrow.
> It exposes our innermost thoughts and desires.
> (Heb 4:12)

What two things does the word of God expose? Your thoughts and desires. To whom does it expose our inner life? To you, yourself. How do you feel when Scripture works on your inner self? Painful, like being cut by a sharp sword. How aggressive is Scripture in performing such heart surgery on you? It is living and moving and powerfully searching both your mind for loose thoughts as well as your heart for ungodly desires.

If your thoughts and desires are not regularly challenged by God's Spirit at work in you through God's word, what does that indicate? It could be one of three things: One option: You are not in the word of God as you should be. Another possibility: You are intentionally grieving God's Spirit by ignoring what he is trying to do in you. A third consideration: Could it be that you have never surrendered yourself to the Lordship of Christ?

> *Are you praying God's word back to him?*

Take the time right now, before moving on through the rest of this chapter, to consider how often and how easily the Spirit of God uses the word of God to challenge your thoughts and desires. What will you do to give the Spirit more freedom to change your inner man? Needed: a living, active, heart-changing dialogue with God concerning your thoughts and desires.

If you have surrendered the leadership of your life over to the Lordship of Christ, then being in God's word is the first step. Praying God's word back to him is the second.

When you make a habit of praying God's Word back to him, you will find yourself more able to discern what thoughts are of God and what thoughts are not. You will see your own motives and desires as you truly are, no longer deceiving yourself. You will be instantly refreshed as the authority of God's Word dispels the darkness in your mind. You will be empowered daily to develop the mind of Christ.[2]

God's word is one weapon. Prayer is another weapon. When we pray God's word, we use two powerful weapons at the same time.

> *Praying God's word helps you see your life from God's perspective.*

---

2. One of the best books I can recommend to you is T.W. Hunt's book, "The Mind of Christ."

Whoopin' Up on Stinkin' Thinkin'

We use the truth of God's word to shatter deceptive thoughts implanted in our minds. We use prayer to get God in on our self-talk, a realm where, without prayer, Satan often has free reign.

When you pray God's word, you are firing God's double-barrel power at the enemy. Having one barrel is good. Having a double-barrel weapon is even better. Having a super-charged, double-barrel weapon with an unceasing supernatural supply of ammunition spells v-i-c-t-o-r-y! Try this for victory over a stronghold:

- Pray honestly for insight into what strongholds trouble you.
- Memorize verses in God's word that specifically address your stronghold.
- Let the meaning of the verses inspire your thoughts and become your prayer.
- Based on the verses, ask God what thoughts and desires need to change.
- When stinkin' thinkin' happens, repeat the verse aloud.
- Engage God in dialogue, speaking his own word back to him, saying that particular personalized verse aloud.
- When praying the Word, personalize the words to say "I" in reference to self, and "you" in place of references to God.
- Tell God that you are no longer in agreement with the darkness of deception. You are in agreement with the specific truth in that particular verse.
- Repeat as often as needed. Mental strongholds can be stubborn.

New Testament believers quoted God's word back to him as they prayed. When Peter and John were released from questioning, they returned back to the group of Christ followers. All the believers listened to what had happened to Peter and John, and then they lifted up their voices in prayer. Notice the source of their prayer:

> O Sovereign Lord . . .
> You spoke long ago by the Holy Spirit
> through our ancestor David, your servant, saying,
> "Why were the nations so angry? . . .
> The kings of the earth prepared for battle . . .

The Ultimate Whoopin'!

> against his Messiah."
> In fact, this has happened here
> in this very city! . . .
> And now, oh Lord, hear their threats . . .
> (Acts 4:24–29)

As these early followers of Christ prayed, they quoted God's word back to him, citing the second psalm, where a prophecy is made of Christ. The word of God was already hidden in their hearts, and they were looking at their current circumstances through the lens of Scripture. Praying the word of God back to the Lord helps us put our lives into God's scriptural perspective.

New Testament Christianity gives us a pattern for . . .

- interpreting our current situation in light of specific truth already revealed to us in Scripture
- quoting that Scripture back to God as we talk to him about our lives.

I can think of no more powerful way to change the way you think than to pray God's word back to him.[3] Praying Scripture can feel a bit awkward at first. Personalizing the verses takes truth from the conceptual level to the place where faith meets life, which means we have to decide whether or not we are serious about letting God change our lives.

> *Are you praying God's word back to him?*

I challenge you to give it a try! Take the risk. Press through the early awkwardness and get accustomed to speaking God's word back to him. Learn to pray his word in a very powerful, personalized way.

Here are some examples of how praying God's word can give you victory over spiritual strongholds. Let these short starter-prayers serve to help you build an armory of prayer through using multiple verses in your fight for victory over the enemy. Take this as a challenge to search the Scriptures for yourself to find God's truth for your life situation.

---

3. An excellent resource for praying God's word, whether you are male or female, is Beth Moore's book, "Praying God's Word: Breaking Free From Spiritual Strongholds"

Whoopin' Up on Stinkin' Thinkin'

Stinkin' Thinkin'	Praying God's Word
Something bad is about to happen. I can feel it. (Fear)	God, I am strong and courageous. I am not afraid or discouraged. For you, Lord God, are with me wherever I go (Josh 1:9).
Strongly divided opinions around me make me unable to rest. I'm troubled. (Anxiety)	Lord, you left me with a gift; peace of mind and heart. The peace you give is a gift the world cannot give. So I will not be troubled or afraid (John 14:27).
I don't really belong anywhere. (Loneliness)	Lord, to all who believe in you and accept you, you give the right to become your children. I belong to you (John 1:12)! You decided in advance to adopt me into your family by bringing me to Christ Jesus (Eph 1:5).
I don't have a family. (Isolation, lack of acceptance)	Lord, you say in your word that all the members of Christ's body care for each other. If one suffers, we all suffer, and if one is honored, we are all honored. I belong to your family. Help me open up myself to my brothers and sisters. Help me care about them as well (1 Cor 12:24–27).
I am just a sinner, saved by grace. There's nothing special about me. (Insignificance)	Lord, I agree with Matthew 5:13, that says, I am the salt of the earth, and Ephesians 2:9, that says I am your masterpiece, created anew in Christ Jesus so I can do good things you planned for me long ago.
I just can't get over what all I've done to hurt others. (Guilt)	Lord, you say in Colossians 1:14 that you purchased my freedom from guilt and forgave my sins. I am in Christ Jesus, and you say in Romans 8:1–2 there is no condemnation over me.
I feel like God has forgotten about me. He no longer has a plan for me. (Abandonment)	Father, I agree with your word in Philippians 1:6 that I am certain that since you began this good work in me, you will continue your work until it is finished.
I will never be able to forgive what was done to me. (Unforgiveness)	Lord, you say in 2 Corinthians 2:7–11 that it is time for me to forgive and even comfort the one I have wanted to hurt. I do so with Christ's authority, knowing Satan's evil scheme to keep me in the bondage of bitterness. As I forgive others, forgive me (Matt 6:12).
Oh Lord, I am so quick to notice the faults of others, and so eager to overlook my own. (Pride)	Father, your word says that you oppose the proud and give grace to the humble (Jas 4:6). Humble me. I don't want your opposition. I want your grace. I humble myself before you, Lord (Jas 4:10).

The Ultimate Whoopin'!

Other people may think of what I have as a stronghold, but I *need* it to live. (Self-deception over addiction or idolatry)	Lord, you say in Psalm 51:6 that you desire truth in my inner most parts. Teach me wisdom in my inmost places. As you say in Romans 1:25, I have exchanged your truth for a lie. You warn me not to be deceived (Jas 1:16). Show me my self-deception. Set me free.
God made me the way I am. It's alright that I meet my body's needs, one way or the other. (Lust)	Lord, I agree with your word in Romans 1:24–25 that I have given myself over to the sexual desires of my body. I have degraded myself by sexual impurity. If I remain unrepentant, I am storing up wrath for myself (Rom 2:5–10).
There is a darkness in me that I just can't get away from. (Spiritual oppression)	Lord, I *claim* to be in harmony with Jesus, yet it seems like Satan has my soul. I agree with your word in 2 Corinthians 6:15; what harmony can there be between Christ and the devil? Lord, show me how I have compromised with Satan. I claim the promise of Colossians 2:13–15 that on the cross, Jesus disarmed any evil power over me.
I must _____ in order to feel good about myself (fill in the blank: look good, make more money, be liked, whatever). (Performance-based self-worth)[1]	Lord, I have this seemingly chronic urge to prove my worth to myself and to others. I have allowed human opinion of me to rule my life. You say in Colossians 2:10 that I am complete through my union with Christ. In Christ I am accepted as Christ's friend (John 15:15). I am secure in whose I am (Col 3:3). I am significant (Eph 2:6).
There is only so much good. If good happens to others, it takes away potential good I could have received. God is stingy. (Limited good concept)	Lord, I have put you in a small box, forgetting how big and powerful you are. Show me the truth of Ephesians 3:20. You are able through your mighty power at work in us to do infinitely more than we might ask or think. With you, there is unlimited good. Wow!
People don't pay attention to me as they should. To get people moving, I have to get angry.	God, you say in Proverbs 29:11 that if I lose my temper, I am a fool. Forgive me. You get my attention through your never-ending, undeserved love for me. John 13:35 says the only way people will know I am your child is if I show them your love, not my anger. Help me move people with kindness.

4. I recommend "The Search for Significance," by Robert McGee, for those who struggle with self-identity.

Whoopin' Up on Stinkin' Thinkin'

THE ULTIMATE WHOOPIN'

Questions for Reflection and Discussion

1. Read Hebrews 4:12.
   What two things does the Word of God expose?

   To whom does it expose our inner life?

   How do you feel when Scripture works on your inner man?

   How aggressive is Scripture in performing such heart surgery on you?

   If your thoughts and desires are not regularly challenged by God's Spirit at work in you through God's word, what might that indicate?

2. Read 2 Timothy 3:16.
   What does Scripture most need to do within you now?
   ___ show you truth, exposing your self-deception
   ___ cause you to admit areas of rebellion
   ___ correct your stinkin' thinkin' about _____
   ___ train you daily in living obedient to Christ

3. Review the chart of examples of praying God's word over strongholds. Identify a few strongholds in your mind, some of which may not appear on the chart. Search the Scripture and pray God's word back to him to begin reclaiming every part of your mind as Christ's territory.

Stinkin' Thinkin'	Praying God's Word

4. Who should you tell about your battle with these strongholds? God will begin breaking down your strongholds through even just one authentic relationship in which you are transparent with each other.

*Think about the things
of heaven,
not the things of earth.
For you died to this life,
and your real life
is hidden with Christ in God.*

Colossians 3:2–3 NLT

---

*Since you have heard about Jesus
and have learned the truth
that comes from him,
throw off your old sinful nature and
your former way of life,
which is corrupted by
lust and deception.
Instead, let the Spirit renew
your thoughts and attitudes.*

Ephesians 4:21–23 NLT

11

Getting High on Elevated Thinking

A MAN FOUND AN eagle's egg and put it into the nest of a prairie chicken. The eaglet hatched with a brood of chicks and grew up with them. Thinking he was a prairie chicken, he did what prairie chickens do. He clucked and he cackled. Sometimes he flapped his wings and went just a few feet off the ground. Most days he spent his time scratching in the dirt looking for seeds and insects. After all, that's what prairie chickens do.

The years passed by, and the eaglet slowly grew old. One day, he saw a magnificent bird soaring far above in a clear blue sky. He watched the graceful creature glide, soaring majestically on strong wings.

To a neighbor, he said, "What in the world is that? Wow!"

"That's an eagle. The eagle is the greatest of all birds. But it's not for you to think about. You could never be like an eagle."

So the eagle never gave it a second thought. He died, thinking he was a chicken. *Stinkin' thinkin!*

What were the chances of the eagle changing his behavior if he didn't change his thinking?

What *stinkin' thinkin'* has you clucking and scratching the ground like a prairie chicken?

While the doctrine of the total depravity of man's sinful state is true, in some circles it has been exclusively emphasized without much talk of grace and the possibility of becoming a new creation in Christ. The result is that

Whoopin' Up on Stinkin' Thinkin'

many Christ followers are mentally stuck in the rut of only looking at their own sin, while their new nature in Christ is not realized.

Do you often think, "Who am I to attempt great things for God? I'm just a wormlike sinner, barely saved by grace." *Stinkin' thinkin'*! The truth is that God wants the one who serves him to fly like an eagle. The one who waits on the Lord soars on wings as an eagle (Isa 40:31). What *stinkin' thinkin'* is keeping you on the ground?

God wants to lift us up as his people and raise us to an elevated way of thinking. However, there are mental strongholds keeping us from soaring like eagles. Before we can fly, we must take a look to see if there are rocks tied to our legs, keeping us on the ground. Here are some things to consider in that regard:

Stop to actually examine the things on which your mind dwells. Do you discover that you are often playing mental trivial pursuit, rehearsing unimportant things? Do you find that your thoughts gravitate toward frustration, anger, and meanness?

> *Do you make heroes out of people with no admirable virtue?*

Does your thought process end up depressing and demotivating you? Does your mind make heroes out of people who, though they may be popular, powerful, or pretty, have no admirable *virtue*? Do you find yourself regularly tearing down self and others?

Those who soar through life as God's eagles were not just randomly placed up in the jet stream. They soar even though many things could have kept them on the ground. They mount up with wings as eagles because they have learned to wait on the Lord, and he has given them his perspective on life. He has given them his mind.

Like the heavens are far above the earth, so God's thoughts are way higher than our thoughts (Isa 55:9). We tend to see only the plow in our hands. God sees the entire field, the surrounding fields, the topography in every direction, the unknown natural spring water within the earth beneath our feet, the agricultural effects of the atmosphere above us, the neighbors who could become plowing partners with us, and even the future level of demand for our crop. God's thinking is all-encompassing.

Once you and I as earth dwellers begin to see our lives from God's higher perspective, we realize how much God is at work behind the scenes causing us to reap a harvest in life. We see that life is way bigger than simply

Getting High on Elevated Thinking

keeping our hands on the plow. When we develop his perspective, his way of thinking, he lifts us up to soar far above, where we can see the field of our lives as he does.

Seeing life from God's vantage point might be compared to the elation of riding a hot-air balloon over the place where you live. The view not only gives you a totally new perspective, it is exhilarating. It's time we started getting high on elevated thinking!

Par for the course, God leaves no guesswork when helping us learn how to think. In his word, he provides precision points to ponder as we elevate our minds.

> And now dear brothers and sisters, one final thing.
> Fix your thoughts on what is true, and honorable,
> and right, and pure, and lovely, and admirable.
> Think about things that are
> excellent and worthy of praise.
> (Phil 4:8)

The word "think" in Philippians 4:8 is the Greek word *logizomai*. We get our word logic from this word. *Logizomai* is an accounting term. It is used when keeping accounting records, to determine whether or not an item should be considered as legitimate. It means to count as legitimate.

Your brain is like an accounting record. Your brain constantly needs to balance its mental checkbook. If illegitimate thoughts are placed into the account record, the entire record becomes inaccurate. The brain cannot relax because it is out of balance. There is no peace of mind. When that happens, you as the accountant must search for the inaccurate items in your way of thinking and remove them. Your mental account will then balance and your mind will be at peace.

Some of your thoughts may be throwing your life off kilter! Search for those thoughts and remove them, so you will be thinking accurately and living in the jet stream of elevated thinking.

How ready are you to soar into elevated thinking? Here are eight standards to test whether your mind is where it should be.

Whoopin' Up on Stinkin' Thinkin'

THE REALITY TEST:
AM I DWELLING ON REAL TRUTH?

> And now dear brothers and sisters, one final thing.
> Fix your thoughts on what is true . . .
> (Phil 4:8)

Satan is a deceiver. He wants to corrupt your mental accounting with half-truths, throwing off your bottom line balance. He says, "You are a bird, yes that is true. The kind of bird you are is called 'prairie chicken.' You know that, don't you?" He subtly gets you thinking in half-truths.

"I can't be expected to accomplish things more difficult than what I am already doing. I have so many faults and limitations." *Stinkin' prairie chicken thinkin'.*

Sometimes the deceiver gets you thinking more of yourself than you ought. "I can soar so high, there is no one higher than me. I am the sovereign one controlling my own destiny." *Stinkin' prideful thinkin'.*

Other times, the deception comes in very modern, sophisticated-sounding ideology. "There is no one-size-fits-all 'truth.' What's true for you may not be true for me."

Let's put that to the test. On the count of three, let's all jump up. One. Two. Three. Jump! Did you come back down? I did as well. If you did not come back down, please raise your hand. Seeing no hands, we know that what was true for one of us was true for all of us, was it not?

Here's another test. The last time you were physically cut deep into your flesh, did you bleed? Are there any of you reading this who did not bleed when you were cut deeply? What is true for one of us is true for all of us.

"Truth is relative." *Stinkin' relativism thinkin'.*

If there is such a thing as unchanging, ultimate Truth, how can we know it? If a thought is considered to be true, it must pass the test of whether or not it conforms to Ultimate Reality, which is God the truth, incarnated in Christ Jesus. He is *the* truth. He not only *told* the truth. He *lived* the truth. He not only lived the truth, he himself *is* the Truth. Jesus is the ultimate reality by which everything must be tested to verify its truthfulness.

Where do you find the detailed truths comprising Ultimate Truth? You find them in the teachings of Christ. Jesus said, "I am the way, the truth, and the life. No one can come to the Father except though me" (John

14:6). Without him, there is no going (the way). Without him, there is no knowing (the truth). Without him, there is no living (the life).

God's world is based on truth, which makes it perfect and beautiful. Since the fall of man into sin (Gen 2), life on this planet has been based on deception. This earth, to which the Lord willingly descended, has become stained with sin. The coming of Jesus from heaven to earth was a truth invasion. Jesus brought teaching that was, in actuality, out of this world. The result was a truth encounter; a clashing of two incompatible worlds.

> *Jesus invaded this planet to create a different world . . . and a different you!*

Jesus' invasion of earth was for the purpose of creating a very different world than the one you and I know. His truth is intended to recreate this world to be perfect and beautiful, like heaven. He intends, through his truth, to create a very different you. To enter into God's world, a transformation is required; an invasion of Jesus into your soul, body, heart, and psyche.

Are you able to discern which of your thoughts pair with Ultimate Reality and which do not? When you pair your phone with the Bluetooth in a car, data is shared and invisible communication begins without ceasing. The car takes over control of the phone.

Pair your mind with the mind of Christ. Ask Christ to share his data with you. Let him invade you. Give Christ freedom to control your life. He will transform you, starting with the way you think.

What percent of your mental processing is spent thinking on the teachings of Christ? Let's say you spend two hours a week at church. The rest of your waking time totals approximately 110 hours. What do you think about during those waking hours?

Are you dwelling on truth? As you explore the red letters of Christ's words, create some practical means to help you dwell on his truths. Put post-it notes of meaningful sayings of Christ on your fridge. Create reminders on your phone that will pop up, calling to mind Christ's truths. Set a regular time and place to meet with someone, with both of you agreeing the sole agenda will be to refresh each other on truth from the word of God.

Instead of adding another weekly TV program to your viewing, spend that time walking outside meditating on God's word. Carry Scripture memory cards in your pocket, and pull them out every time you sip a drink.

What creative thing will you do to dwell on real truth?

Take the reality test: Ask yourself, *Am I dwelling on thoughts that are true?*

Fix your thoughts on what is true.

THE NOBILITY TEST: AS GOD'S AMBASSADOR, ARE MY THOUGHTS HONORABLE?

> And now dear brothers and sisters, one final thing.
> Fix your thoughts on what is . . . honorable . . .
> (Phil 4:8)

The word honorable carries with it the idea of being weighty, having a sense of decorum, that which is of significant substance. Honor is the aura of dignity radiating from an ambassador representing a king.

You represent the King of kings and Lord of lords! You are his ambassador. Your thoughts should be worthy of the One you serve. To act and think like his ambassador, you must meet with him regularly and get to know his mind. You must engrain in your psyche the reality that everything you think and do reflects on him.

After university graduation, Marilyn spent two years as a missionary in what was then the territory of Hawaii. One Sunday night while she was teaching at church, a marine in uniform walked in, and she was so enthralled with him she lost her train of thought.

It wasn't long before that marine asked to kiss her. She promptly replied, "Oh, I can't do that. I work for God!" She did eventually kiss that marine, but only after calling home and getting her father's permission! Now that's noble, honorable thinking!

That kiss set off a series of events which gave me my wonderful wife! My mother-in-law, Marilyn, has now been honorably promoted to heaven.

Do we think on honorable thoughts? So many times our thoughts are simply not worth the brainpower we allow them to consume. The mind makes up less than 5 percent of our body mass, but consumes over 20 percent of our calories! What in the world are we thinking about to burn up all that

> *Does your cell cause you to chase virtual rabbits and miss out on a life of real substance?*

energy? How much of our thought life is spent on electronic devices, chasing virtual rabbits?

Hmm. I'll check the weather app, to see if I can exercise outdoors after work. Oh, there's the investment app. Let me see if things are up or down today. Oh, look what popped up! That's the fashion trending these days? Who wears that? Here comes a Facebook update. Wow! Lots of people are responding to that one. Who is that person? Let me take a look at her profile . . .

Though such entertainment keeps you mentally occupied, it can also easily distract you from thinking about things of real substance. Chasing virtual rabbits can keep you from interacting with real people right around you. Most tragically, social media can easily draw your attention to the seemingly perfect identity of others while possibly causing you to forget your own identity as Christ's ambassador.

Have you stopped to think about the way you use social media? Is it honorable? How could you use social media in more honorable ways? Here's one way. Try placing a social media update that prompts dialogue about noble things of true substance. For instance, you could post the words of Philippians 4:8, and ask people to respond with which part of such elevated thinking they find easiest and what part they find most difficult.

Take the nobility test: *As God's ambassador, do my thoughts honor the One I represent?*

Fix your thoughts on what is honorable.

THE VIRTUE TEST: ARE MY THOUGHTS IN KEEPING WITH GOD'S RIGHTEOUS STANDARDS?

> And now dear brothers and sisters, one final thing.
> Fix your thoughts on what is . . . right . . .
> (Phil 4:8)

The word "right" describes that which meets with God's moral approval. Our human nature makes us prone to live by the approval of others. Intentionally living for God's approval means living counter-culturally. In a world of moral relativism, where most people's thoughts are fixed on doing what is right in their *own* minds, the challenge we face is to devote our minds toward knowing and doing what is right in *God's* sight.

Whoopin' Up on Stinkin' Thinkin'

There is such confusion these days on morality. I was with a group of Christian men who were talking about their teenage sons. To my surprise, they agreed with each other that they wanted their sons to experience sex before marriage. Whatever happened to the godly truth that true love should wait?

Pornography also seems to be accepted now as normal. Dirty internet usage is on the rise. Vance Havner said, "Never since Manhattan Island sold for twenty-four dollars has so much dirt been available so cheap!"[1]

> *Put away thoughts that add a scowl to your face. Dwell on thoughts that make you attractive.*

God does not put in place righteous standards for the purpose of taking away all human fun. A fence around a playground is not designed to keep children from playing and having fun. It is designed to keep children safe as they play.

God places fences around you for you to be able to experience freedom, knowing that you are remaining safe within his boundaries. Outside of his righteous fences, danger lurks.

As you stay within God's moral fences, you position yourself to be blessed with the confidence that you are pleasing God. You are doing what is right in his sight, regardless of what others may do. Keep your mind stayed on him, and you will find yourself trusting his standard of right and wrong. The result will be a deeply settled peace within you (Isa 26:3).

Take the virtue test: *God, are my thoughts in keeping with your righteous standards?*

Fix your thoughts on what is right.

THE CLEAN TEST: IS MY THOUGHT LIFE PURE?

> And now dear brothers and sisters, one final thing.
> Fix your thoughts on what is . . . pure . . .
> (Phil 4:8)

The word "purity" comes from the same root word as the word holy. It means set apart for God's use. The word picture is that of a vessel cleansed, ready to be presented to God in worship. Fix your thoughts only on things that would be acceptable before God. Set apart your mind for God's use.

---

1. Revivalsermons.org

God created sex to bless husbands and wives within marriage. However, much of sex on television is outside of marriage, and is made to look glamorous and desirable.[2] Adultery begins in the mind and heart. Guard your heart. Guard your mind.

You are a temple of God's Spirit. God himself dwells within the follower of Christ. Let your mind be unadulterated. Make no room for dirty-mindedness. Allow no impure mental input from TV, cell phone, friends, computer, or ear buds. Let no spoiled, contaminated thinking be a part of who you are.

You can choose what you think about. When a thought first comes to mind, ask yourself, "Could I bring this thought before God in an act of worship?"

What are pure things you can think about? God's unconditional agape love is pure. The life of Christ on earth was 100 percent pure, without sin. The word of God is pure, without any mixture of error. A faithful marriage is pure, undefiled before God. Godly friendships can be pure. Most dogs seem to me to be pure. Cats, not so much. Heaven will be wholly pure.

Take the clean test: *Is my thought life pure?*

Fix your mind on whatever is pure.

THE LOVABILITY TEST:
DO MY THOUGHTS MAKE ME A LOVELY PERSON?

> And now dear brothers and sisters, one final thing.
> Fix your thoughts on what is . . . lovely . . .
> (Phil 4:8)

The word lovely means that which inspires love. It refers to something being lovable. We are told to fix our thoughts on things that turn us into lovable people.

Right away, we know that some thoughts make us unlovable, such as envy, hatred, greed, a critical spirit, gossip, and bitterness. Learn to put away thoughts that add a scowl to your face. Fix your mind on thoughts that make your face want to be looked at. Dwell on thoughts that make you attractive from the inside out. Become someone people want to emulate because of your winsome thinking.

---

2. https://afajournal.org/1996/0396AFAJ.pdf

Whoopin' Up on Stinkin' Thinkin'

During my university days, I majored in public speech. Dr. Dorothy Nell Rogers was my primary professor. She embodied the thought life described in Philippians 4:8. Sometimes, she would tilt her head back as if mentally leaving this world and become completely quiet.

She would pause for quite some time, and then she would describe an event or a person to inspire us toward lofty thinking. Though she had the toughest expectations of any teacher I've ever had, she was an absolutely lovable person. She fixed her mind on things that were lofty and lovely. Men, to become winsome, think attractive thoughts. Ladies, to be a lovable person, think lovely thoughts.

What are some lovable things to think about? The Heavenly Father is overflowing with love. You have family members who love you. There are puppy dogs ready to lick you. Outside is a big beautiful world full of sunshine and rain, blizzards and deserts, mountains and valleys. It's a diverse, beautiful world in which we live. You gotta love it. Go out and enjoy God's creation. It will make you winsome and lovable.

You can choose to dwell on the ugly. You can focus on all the world's terrible problems. You can commiserate on everyone who's ever wronged you. Do all that unlovely thinking, and your face will begin to scowl and have worry wrinkles, repelling people away from you. Your face slowly molds itself to your thoughts. As for me, I want a face that radiates with God's glory. I chose to dwell on winsome, lovely things.

Ladies, take the lovability test: *Do my thoughts make me a lovely lady?*

Men, take the attractive test: *Do my thoughts make me a winsome winner?*

Fix your thoughts on what is lovely.

THE REPUTATION TEST: IF PEOPLE COULD READ MY MIND, WOULD I GET A GOOD REPORT?

> And now dear brothers and sisters, one final thing.
> Fix your thoughts on what is . . . admirable . . .
> (Phil 4:8)

The word "admirable" means spoken highly of, well reported, and reputable. Being admirable comes, in part, from admiring notable character traits in others, which inspires you to develop such traits yourself.

Getting High on Elevated Thinking

Who you do look up to? Who do you think about as someone worth emulating? Among those you know, who is truly an inspiring person? Start asking around about followers of Christ who inspire others. Find people locally and digitally who are worthy of admiration; people who are true heroes. Fill your mind with the lives of truly inspiring people!

I have read dozens of books on the lives of godly people that have challenged me to develop the qualities I see in them. To help you fix your mind on admirable people and their godly character, let me recommend three volumes to you. Each volume is a collection of biographies of inspiring people. These stories share the imperfections of the people as well, which seems to cause the overwhelmingly admirable part of their lives to shine even brighter.

I am currently rereading *From Jerusalem to Irian Jaya*, by Ruth Tucker. This great work is a concise biographical history of Christian missions. I love this book, and have taught seminary and university students much of its content. In my current reread, I am moving through it as slowly as possible, because I will be sad when I no longer have another admirable life to read about.

Preacher and writer Warren Wiersbe has put together a book called *50 People Every Christian Should Know*. Most of the people featured are pastors, evangelists, and Christian authors. When you read this book, you will find yourself making a list of other books to buy. You will meet stimulating people you never knew existed. You will be inspired to think on what is admirable.

> *Who are your heroes? Choose them carefully!*

Regardless of your theological bent, for those seeking to have a mind fixed on what is admirable, John Piper's biographical history of the Reformation is a must read. The title is *21 Servants of Sovereign Joy*. For twenty-one years, John preached a different biographical sermon every year to a pastor's conference, and the result is this voluminous yet worthwhile book.

Too often we seek merely to *appear* as someone who is admirable. Such a shallow goal can be accomplished through deceptive social media postings. However, God knows the true condition of our hearts and so do those closest to us. The goal is to think admirable thoughts simply for the benefit of having a wholesome, healthy mind, even if no one else notices.

Take the reputation test: *If people could read my mind, would I get a good report on what I am thinking?*

Fix your mind on what is admirable.

The Uplifting Test: Does Dwelling on My Current Thoughts Help Me Toward Godly Excellence?

> And now dear brothers and sisters, one final thing.
> Fix your thoughts on what is . . . excellent . . .
> (Phil 4:8)

Though the word "excellent" in this verse has many nuances, it means that which enriches life, that which adds value or virtue.

Even if something is factually true, it doesn't mean that it is worth your brainpower. Is a particular thought helpful, to you and to others? Does it move you and others toward best practices? Is it something you would want your pastor, your momma, or your child to know about? Does it move you toward higher places?

Pastor Charles Swindoll had his oil changed in his truck. He watched the mechanic take off an underneath section that he'd never seen taken off before.

Chuck asked the mechanic what he was doing. After fully removing the gunky cover, the man replied, "This ought to be taken off and cleaned every ten thousand miles."

"No one will ever see it."

"I will."

Excellence made a loyal customer out of Swindoll.[3]

Don't just think about what it will take to meet the minimum requirements. Don't just mentally clock in and then mentally clock out when the job is pretty much done. Dress your mind for top-notch success. Sharpen your mind to follow through on every detail to the full completion of the project. Take the time to back up and make needed changes so the result goes from good to great.

> *One day God will evaluate the return he got from investing into your life.*

Think about how you can glorify God and bless others by doing your very best, by raising the bar of expectation, and by providing the highest possible return on God's investment in your life.

---

3. See "Swindoll's Ultimate Book of Illustrations and Quotes," p. 186.

Getting High on Elevated Thinking

Jesus told a story about what the end times will be like. He told of an owner who went on a trip. He left one steward five bags of coins, another steward two bags, and a third steward one bag.

When he returned, the five-bagger had invested wisely and had ten bags. The two-bagger had four, while the one-bagger still had only one dusty little bag. The owner commended the two stewards who had invested well, yet told the steward who buried the one bag that he was evil and lazy (Matt 25:14–30).

God is your owner. You are his steward. A day is coming at the end of time when your Owner will evaluate the return he gets from his investment into your life.

Regardless of how much he has entrusted to you, he expects that until he returns, you will do your very best to give him a good return on his investment.

What on earth are you living for? *Figure out God's personalized plan for your life and give it all you've got!* Refuse merely to exist. Serve the Lord by caring for others extravagantly. Creatively consider what talents and gifts you have and how you can use them for God. Leverage your spiritual influence on others to make the highest impact possible. Take whatever resources God has entrusted to you, and maximize your active investment of each and every coin.

Don't just let money sit in a bank. Study investing methods and get the money growing so you can . . .

thrive instead of survive,
be blessed instead of stressed,
and give instead of gripe.

If you average growth of 12 percent per year on investments, the coins you manage for him will double every six years.

"Oh, but God has only given me one bag of coins." *Stinkin' thinkin'.*

Even if you are "just" a one-bagger, do the math. In thirty years at 12 percent per year, you could turn one bag of coins into thirty-two bags, and in sixty years, one bag would become 1,024 bags of coins! God is expecting a good return on his investment into your life. Live with excellence!

Clean out the cobwebs in the unused corners of your mind and bring forth the most creative thinking you have. Expand your areas of reading. Develop diligent thinking that looks at every angle of the situation, so as not to be surprised by the amount of effort involved or by obstacles.

Most importantly, practice your best thinking so you don't miss out on opportunities overlooked by mediocre thinkers. Strive to be the very best *you*, for the sake of hearing, at the Master's return, "Well done, my good and faithful servant."

Take the uplifting test: *Does dwelling on my current thoughts lift me up toward godly excellence?*

Fix your mind on things of excellence.

THE COMMENDATION TEST: DOES MY MIND LOOK FOR WHAT IS PRAISEWORTHY?

> And now dear brothers and sisters, one final thing.
> Fix your thoughts on what is . . . worthy of praise.
> (Phil 4:8)

In this world filled with so much negative thinking, it's easy to forget that God wants us as his people to mount up with wings like eagles and soar. It's so easy to fall into *stinkin' prairie chicken thinkin'*.

Guard your mind against thought patterns that demotivate, darken, and depress. Mental strongholds often develop from spending time with negative people. Even within the body of Christ, you must guard against those who deceive themselves into believing they have the spiritual gifts of criticism, gossip, and gloom. You don't need negative people's thoughts bringing your eagle flight down.

If God is worthy of all your praise, then you should fill your mind with his praise, to the point where your body cannot help but follow biblical commands such as lifting your hands, clapping your hands, shouting to the Lord, and bowing before him. Dance before the Lord if you feel like it. Soar with praise, my friend, soar!

Here's a challenge. Get alone in your own space and listen to praise music as loud as you like. Buy new speakers if needed. Sing along loud enough so that the dog next door starts to howl along with you. You will soar in your spirit!

Let your mind climb up to a lofty verse of Scripture by saying it aloud over and over until you are saying it from your heart without looking at it. Visualize in your mind how that verse is changing your thoughts and your life.

Getting High on Elevated Thinking

Call five friends and say to each one, "Tell me something good God is doing in your life right now," then listen carefully and rejoice with them. Wait for them to ask you, and then tell each of them how good God is being toward you. Do whatever it takes to get your mind racing with inspiration to the point of elation, shouting, weeping, kneeling, jumping, or simply being still and knowing that he is God.

Sure, you could develop the ability of seeing the faults in just about everyone and in nearly every situation. Of course, you could pride yourself by pointing out the shortcomings of others and poking holes in people's plans. Are those skills you want on your resume? Why be like that, when you are an eagle designed to soar? Find what is worthy of commendation, not condemnation.

Think on the praiseworthy qualities you see in other people. Always believe in others. Trust others. Look for the best in others. Read the life of Christ, and notice how he saw the best in a fraudulent tax collector, a demon-possessed man, an adulterer, and nearly everyone he met.[4]

Be ready to forgive seventy times seven. There's something good to say about every single person on this planet, because God created each of us, and God don't make no junk! Don't ever give up on *anyone*. God is all about changing people. Yes, he can even change that person who just came to your mind! Look what he's done with *you*!

Take the commendation test: *Does my mind look for what is worthy of praise?* Let your mind dwell on what is praiseworthy. The high road of lofty living is available to those with the mind of Christ.

While studying these chapters together over a period of several months in home groups, the people of Oakhill Baptist Church of Austin shared their hearts with each other. One evening, we split up by gender, with the women going to the theater room upstairs and the men staying in the family room downstairs.

The men started talking about guy stuff. Soon the mood became more serious as we discussed the challenges of avoiding sexual temptations. Every man there talked about the challenges of pornography, workplace flirting, and inner urges.

After a while, Rob spoke up. He said, "I find the best way to avoid temptation is not by focusing on it but by focusing on my wife. She is

---

4. Here's the exception: Jesus saw the hypocrisy of religious people who thought themselves better than others (Pharisees), and he was indignant toward them.

wonderful, and I want to be a blessing to her every day with what I think, say, and do. I want to cherish her, and be a real one-woman man for her."

Accountability groups often ask very specific questions to make sure group members have not given in to temptation. Christian accountability groups tend to focus on not committing sin, instead of developing virtue. Elevated thinking, on the other hand, focuses on developing the virtue of wanting to bless your spouse with words, deeds, gifts, and faithfulness.

You become what you think. You can cluck like a chicken, or soar like an eagle. The choice is yours. Which will it be?

GETTING HIGH ON ELEVATED THINKING
Reflection and Discussion

Take the following eight areas of tests, reflecting on the ways that you pass and fail each test.

The reality test: *Am I dwelling on thoughts that are true?*

Possible deceptive thoughts:

Time spent per week on the truths of Christ's teachings:

The nobility test: *As God's ambassador, do my thoughts honor the One I represent?*

Thoughts that might not honor him:

Evaluation of time spent on social media:

Evaluation of purposes behind social media usage:

The virtue test: *Are my thoughts in keeping with God's righteous standards?*

Thoughts of low moral standards:

Ways I am currently trespassing outside God's moral fences:

The clean test: *Is my thought life pure?*

Unclean thoughts I could not bring before God:

For ladies, the lovability test: *Do my thoughts make me a lovely lady?*

Unlovely thoughts:

Whoopin' Up on Stinkin' Thinkin'

For men, the attractive test: *Do my thoughts make me a winsome winner?*

Ugly thoughts:

The reputation test: *If people could read my mind, would I get a good report on what I am thinking?*

Specific people I admire, but should not:

People I should admire, but do not:

The uplifting test: *Does dwelling on my current thoughts lift me up toward godly excellence?*

Mediocre thoughts:

Number of bags of coins I have been given: _____
Number of bags I am turning those into: _____
What the Master will say to me at his return:

The commendation test: *Does my mind look for what is worthy of praise?*

Condemning thoughts:

Overall Grade:
At present, I am . . .
___ still clucking like a chicken, scratching at the ground
___ realizing I am an eagle, but not yet soaring
___ starting to fly like an eagle
___ able to help others soar alongside me
To get to the next level, my most needed mental shift is:

Bibliography

Anderson, Neil T. *The Bondage Breaker: Overcoming Negative Thoughts, Irrational Feelings, & Habitual Sins*. Oxford: Monarch, 2007.

———. *Victory Over the Darkness: Realize the Power of Your Identity in Christ*. Bloomington, MN: Bethany, 2013.

Barna, George. *Turnaround Churches: How to Overcome Barriers to Growth and Bring New Life to an Established Church*. Ventura, CA: Regal, 1993.

Goldwag, Arthur. *Isms & Ologies: All the Movements, Ideologies, and Doctrines That Have Shaped Our World*. New York: Vintage, 2007.

Hunt, T. W. *The Mind of Christ*. Nashville: Broadman & Holman, 1995.

Lewis, C. S. *Mere Christianity*. New York: HarperOne, 2009.

McGee, Robert. *The Search for Significance: Seeing Your True Worth through God's Eyes*. Nashville: Nelson, 2003.

Moore, Beth. *Praying God's Word: Breaking Free from Spiritual Strongholds*. Nashville: B&H, 2018.

Peterson, Eugene H. *The Message: The Bible in Contemporary Language*. Colorado Springs: NavPress, 2005.

Piper, John. *21 Servants of Joy (Complete Set): Faithful, Flawed, and Fruitful*. Wheaton, IL: Crossway, 2018.

Redpath, Alan. *Victorious Christian Living: Studies in the Book of Joshua*. Grand Rapids: Baker, 2013.

Ripken, Nik. *The Insanity of God: A True Story of Faith Resurrected*. Nashville: B&H, 2013.

Swindoll, Charles R. *Swindoll's Ultimate Book of Illustrations & Quotes*. Nashville: Nelson, 2003.

Tucker, Ruth A. *From Jerusalem to Irian Jaya: A Biographical History of Christian Missions*. Grand Rapids: Zondervan, 2004.

Wiersbe, Warren W. *Fifty People Every Christian Should Know*. Grand Rapids: Baker, 2009.

www.ingramcontent.com/pod-product-compliance
Lightning Source LLC
Chambersburg PA
CBHW072134160426
43197CB00012B/2100